Stephen Henry Thayer

Songs of Sleepy Hollow and Other Poems

Stephen Henry Thayer
Songs of Sleepy Hollow and Other Poems
ISBN/EAN: 9783337408053

Printed in Europe, USA, Canada, Australia, Japan

Cover: Foto ©Thomas Meinert / pixelio.de

More available books at **www.hansebooks.com**

STEPHEN HENRY THAYER

SONGS OF SLEEPY HOLLOW

AND

OTHER POEMS

NEW YORK & LONDON
G. P. PUTNAM'S SONS
The Knickerbocker Press
1886

TO

E. F. T.

Long years! and yet they seem like days,
So filled with love's enchanted ways.

These poems have nearly all been published, during the past few years, either in collections or periodicals, and I have thought it only fitting, at the solicitation of numerous friends, to gather them within the bounds of two covers, that they may be preserved for whatever they are worth.

S. H. T.

SLEEPY HOLLOW, *December*, 1885.

CONTENTS.

	PAGE
Solitude	1
The Nyack Bells Heard from Sleepy Hollow	3
Old Sleepy Hollow Church and Irving's Grave	6
In the Pocantico Woods	8
In the Old Sleepy Hollow Cemetery	9
An Old Ruin at Sleepy Hollow	11
The Pocantico in Winter	13
Great Temple of Karnak	15
The Fallen Shaft	16
A Voice from the Sea	17
A June Song	18
Haunted	19
" 'Twas Years Ago "	21
On the Banks of the Souhegan	22
The Death-Roll of Honor	25
Just Beyond	26
Contrasted	28
Two Rivers	30
A Friend	32
March	34
Fare Ye Well	35
Death	36
Faith	37
Matins	38
" The Choir Invisible "	39
A Serenade	40

CONTENTS.

	PAGE
The Secret	42
Uninterpreted	47
Old Hundred	49
Parnassus. William Cullen Bryant	51
L'Avenir	54
A Medley	55
Flood Tide	57
Ah, Could we Know!	58
In Embryo	60
Contrasts—Twilight	61
The Waiting Chords	62
Foreshadowings	64
Voiceless	65
Songs Without Words	67
The Heart of Nature	68
Sanford R. Gifford	70
The Blest	72
"Not Less, But More"	73
Once, a Maiden	75
The Sweet May-Time	77
The First Sorrow	78
Infinito	80
To F. A. H.	81
Betrothed	82
Wedded	83
Presaging	84
The Maid of Another May	85
A Fragment	86
A Song	87
A Song	87
A Parting Song	89
Carlyle	90
Divided	92

CONTENTS.

	PAGE
The Poet's Song	93
Age	96
The Dying Day. To E. S. B.	98
Forget-Me-Nots.	100
"And Give Glad Hearts Their Inning"	101
Clothed Upon	103
From the "Council Ground," Sleepy Hollow	105
A Song Without Words	106
Constancy	107
Thekla	108
"Ah, No More is Love!"	110
In the Ravines of the Catskills	111
Garfield	113
Heart-Possessed	115
Optimism	116
At Length	117
In Memory. F. A. F.—1883	119
September	121
Unexpressed	123
Indian Summer	125
"Ah, Lowly Speaks the Voice of Death!"	127
Heart of Gold	129
Woman-Wise	130
Love's Faith	131
Broken-Hearted	132
Longfellow	134
The Clouded Mind	135
The Mystery	137
1863-1883—Greeting	138
At Sunset. Songs Without Words	139
Fidelity—A Song	140
"Mute Thy Lips"	142
"Sky Top"	143

CONTENTS.

	PAGE
H. W. L. March 24, 1882	145
The Flower and the Tree	146
Seeds, the Engineer	148
Victory	150
November	152
The Old and the New	153
"Give Us, This Day"	155
The Unsent Missive	157
Washington Irving	160
Night-Watches	163
Christmas	163
"The Dead Year"	164
"Abide With Me"	166
Nay, Touch Them Not"	168
Love-Bound	169
Newburgh, October 18, 1883	172
A Challenge to Winter	174
Rest	175
Poet of Earth	176
Grant	177
Prophetic	178
Spirits Anear	179
Past the Portal	180
The Soul of Art	183
Notes	187

SONGS OF SLEEPY HOLLOW.

SOLITUDE.

Wild waters of Pocantico !
   Stray rivulet of wood and glen !
Thy murmuring laughters, soft and low,
   Elude the alien ears of men.

O'er broader bosoms than thine own
   The fleeting wings of commerce glide ;
Hid in thy sylvan haunts alone
   The nymphs of fairy-land abide.

The azure blue of summer's sky
   Scarce mirrors in thy crystal sheen ;
The lover draws his tenderest sigh
   Far in thy shadowy dells unseen.

Along thy gently-coursing stream
   The huntsman, heedless, loves to roam ;
The poet dreams his fondest dream
   Within thy solitary home.

Thou art well guarded by a host,
   For on thy sloping 'bankments stand
Such knarlèd sentinels as boast
   A lineage agèd as the land.

No hardy woodman dare intrude
   To rob thee of thy ancient shade,
Thy mimic cliffs have long withstood
   The furrowing plough and vassal spade.

The wild thrush wings its reedy note
   Through thy lone forest, liquid clear,
Whose answering echoes, far remote,
   Fling back a dim and plaintive cheer.

No tone enslaved in silvery string
   Or sense-enrapturing voice is heard
To match thy melodies, or sing
   A challenge to thy minstrel bird.

Here sovereign Nature teaches rest;
   The quiet mosses on the stone
Weave o'er its silent, flinty breast
   An emerald softness all their own.

The pebbly sands along thy shore
   Lie mutely lulled by babbling waves;

The fringèd fern and gentian flower
  On thy low margin make their graves ;

And through thy valley's dusky shade
  In ceaseless murmurings, ages long,
Shall mingle with the flowers that fade
  Thy endless infancy of song.

O waters of Pocantico !
  Wild rivulet of wood and glen !
May thy glad laughters, sweet and low,
  Long, long outlive the sighs of men !

THE NYACK BELLS HEARD FROM SLEEPY HOLLOW.[1]

The lurking shadows, dim and mute,
  Fall vaguely on the dusky river;
Vexed breezes play a phantom lute
  Athwart the waves that curl and quiver;

And hedged against an amber light,
  The lone hills cling, in vain endeavor
To touch the curtained clouds of night,
  That, weird-like, form and fade forever.

The sad moon bathes with silvery beams
  The hush of twilight-bated breath,

While fallow thoughts, unfathomed dreams,
   Weave mystic webs with life and death.

Then break upon the blessèd calm—
   Deep, dying melodies of even—
Those Nyack bells : like some sweet psalm
   They float along the fields of heaven.

I know not that their liquid knells
   Bear less of joy's than grief's refrain,
Yet from their echoing spirit swells,
   Methinks, a melancholy strain,

As if a throb from out the wave
   Had mingled with their airy motion ;
A song from some fair mermaid's cave ;
   A sigh from some far depth of ocean.

The forests add their sylvan lay ;
   The night-birds lend their plaintive rounds ;
The perfumed flowers that fill the day
   Add incense to the muffled sounds.

And now I hear a marriage chime,
   Commingling with responsive voices ;
A festal song completes the rhyme,
   As heart with wedded heart rejoices.

Then, Lo ! the shadows deepen down,
   And veil in nun-like darkness all ;

THE NYACK BELLS.

Toll slowly, bells, o'er sea and town,
   For death has hung its gloomy pall.

Dark Fancy hears lamenting moans,
   And voices hush, and hearts are broken,
And in thy knells are widowed tones,
   A prayer for some wild woe unspoken.

Then, golden-like, along the west,
   A bright reflection lightens mine,
And visions in my thoughts a rest
   That mingles in these sounds of thine.

Now laden with a nameless balm,
   Now musical with song thou art;
I tune thee by an inward charm,
   And make thee minstrel of my heart.

O bells of Nyack, faintly toll
   Across the starry-lighted sea,
Thy murmurs thrill a thirsty soul
   And wing a heavenly hymn to me.

OLD SLEEPY HOLLOW CHURCH AND IRVING'S GRAVE.

Two centuries have left their hoary trace
Upon yon ancient pile of weathered stone.
Triumphant church ! It stands alone !
Militant no more, nor of the present race.
Its elder saints, called to celestial grace,
No longer now their sins bemoan.

No architectural fancy mars its wall,
Nor modern beauty frets its artless mold ;
The truth is plain, 'tis very old ;
And as I enter through its silent hall,
From faded recollection I recall
The names its history has told.

In imaged thought I seem to see once more,
Around its homely porch and narrow walk,
The sturdy youth in rustic frock ;
And decked in quaintest fashion, as of yore,
Are grouped the maidens round the outer door ;
1 hear the ancient people talk.

Their uncouth dialect, and gestured speech,
Betray the lusty blood of Fatherland.

A stern and pious little band ;
Their simple parson leads to pray and preach ;
They know by heart the lesson he will teach,
And crave a blessing from his hand.

Alas ! the voices which I seem to hear,
Are dreamy echoes of the silent ones ;
I read the churchyard's dingy stones,
The very names sound agèd to the ear,
And half the rude memorials disappear
Where'er the sere gray lichen runs.

Scarce distant from these ancient graves, I turn
And trace the In Memoriam, by the dust
Of one whose pure disdain of lust,
Whose famed yet gentle life no marble urn
Nor bronze recite ; but only hedge and fern
Are wreathed about a nation's trust.

The love a selfish world unselfish bears
Is better left to memory alone ;
No need of praise on mocking stone
Where every passing eye in wonder stares ;
Or, richly blazoned in the city's squares,
Forsooth, to claim what men disown.

Ah ! not the boasting shaft enshrines the man ;
Time has no hour in which to knell the fame

Upborne by an immortal claim ;
For it a bridge ethereal shall span
The ages ; nor the wisest critic's ban,
Nor aught despoil the deathless name.

IN THE POCANTICO WOODS.

What calm is here, what stillness ; every scene
Is eloquent with rest ; the slumbering air
Scarce stirs the whispering foliage. Here and there
A glimmering ray glides, torch-like, in between
The shadowy forms of mossy, mantling green,
And here and there the rivulet's murmurs share
The dreamful solitudes ; 'tis like a prayer !
And far within the forest's emerald screen,
Liquid with music, floats a wingèd song,
Borne on the vibrant odors of a thousand balms.
The world is mute ; it has no blending tone
With nature's symphony, which, deep and strong,
Wooes the worn spirit from illusive charms,
To breathe its speechless longings here alone.

IN THE OLD SLEEPY HOLLOW CEMETERY.

The slab is crumbling fast to dust,
   And, slanting, totters : scarce a trace
Of the quaint carvings, for the rust,
   Is visible across its face.

Death's-head, in dim intaglio, stares
   Through vacant eyes, as if to say,
"I'm dead, I'm one below who shares,
   With others here, the common clay."

The name's obliterated, save
   A skeleton of curve and line :
Like that within the sunken grave,
   It gives no imagery or sign.

And what's the age ? Aye, age indeed !
   A long, long age, for none come here ;
No heart has buried here its need,
   Nor lives a soul to shed a tear.

No deeds by him were done for fame ;
   They all have perished long ago ;

Ah, writ in water was his name;
   His life, his virtues who can know!

No trace is left; nay, say not this,
   If goodness dwelt within his heart,
Then all the coming age is his
   In truths that once he did impart.

As nature's types are wrought from one,
   As spirit unto spirit breathes,
As treasures pass from sire to son,
   So he, unknown, his own bequeathes.

Somewhere existent, incarnate,
   The energy, the will, the life
Of him whose form has met its fate,
   Is mingling with the endless strife.

Somewhere his soul, exultant, shines;
   In other beings fires the blood,
And plans anew in fair designs
   To reach, at last, eternal good.

AN OLD RUIN AT SLEEPY HOLLOW.

Across the brook, above the bridge,
   Crowning, there, a steep ascent,
Stands the ruin on a ridge,
    Shattered, like an old man bent ;
      Solitary, night and day,
      Old, how old no one can say.

Empty, sacked from cell to roof,
   Sunset, through its naked squares,
Glares with lonely gaze, as proof
    That none claim the wreck as theirs,
      Save the dismal bat by day,
      Or the tramp who steals that way.

None its history can tell,
   All its friends are gone or dead ;
Aye, it keeps its secrets well,
    Whispers from its rooms have fled,
      And the legends of its past,
      Mingle with its doom at last.

Who were they that, round its fires,
   Clustered in the days of yore,—

Children and their solemn sires—
  Hundred years ago or more?
  Heroes, or it may be so,
  In the battles long ago.

Ah, if but the silent hearth
  Could discourse of other years,
Or the rafters voice their mirth
  And their murmurs to our ears,
    With what patience would we wait
    For the tales they might relate!

Here, above the ancient clock,
  High along the chimney wall,
Hung, perchance, the old flint-lock,
  Waiting for the signal call,
    Or the Skinner's stealthy tread,
    Listened for in nightly dread.

Here beside the humble board,
  Sober-voiced, with silvered head,
Bowed the old man, uttering, "Lord,
  Give to us our daily bread."
    Pleading, in his simple prayer,
    Blessings on his scanty fare.

Haply pondered here of yore,
  Crooning o'er the swinging crane,
Ichabod, of legend lore,
  Musing, but, alas, in vain,

As he fondly dreamt to mate
His, with fair Katrina's fate.

Many a merry eve, I ween,
   Rustic youth and lass have known
Here, where now, alone, is seen,
   Desolate, the old hearth-stone.
     Many a joy and grief were born
     Here, whence joy and grief are gone.

Ah, the secrets buried here,
   Of the unrecorded dead.
Who, through many a lengthening year,
   Lowly ways of duty led,
     Could we read them, we might trace
Lives that glorified this place.

THE POCANTICO IN WINTER.

The frost has clad thee in an icy shield,
   And thy quick throbs are pent beneath its fold;
Thy gurgling laughter, that through fen and field
   Filled with its ripple many a mossy wold,
Is bound a captive in thy Winter home.
   The birds, blithe spirits of thy sylvan lair,
Who o'er thy Summer solitudes would roam
   In wingèd passion through the scented air,

With plaintive lyrics, long ago took leave ;—
  As friends oft part, with tender notes of song,
Whose hearts, alas! are tuned to sigh and grieve;—
  And thou art left deserted by the throng.
Yet in thy grottoed caves what wild delight!
  'Tis only man who broods in shadow deep,
And glooms his thought with melancholy night ;
  While thou, in thy unquiet prison-keep,

Dost never cease to thrill its crystal wall
  With buoyant eddyings of thy pulsing life,
Till thou shalt rend the bond that holds thee thrall,
  As some glad victor in a merry strife.
E'en now thou hast a dream of murmurous Spring—
  Art fired with fancies of returning bliss,
When balmy airs the waiting buds shall bring,
  And waxing sun shall drink thee with its kiss,—

When veiling mists thy babbling voice shall dim,
  And whispering echoes mock thy lone defiles ;
When hidden springs shall fill thee to the brim,
  And swell thy course to far Elysian isles.
Time has no wizard wand to stem thy love,
  Or woo from thee the witchery of thy spell ;
Thou art a child, perennial, born to rove
  Forever through the same enchanted dell.

And thou shalt sing in thy low, pebbly bed
  Through age on age, unchanged by time's decay ;

While wandering man in circling rounds shall tread
  The troublous earth, and, dying, pass away.
O, lend the heart, thou Melody of Mirth—
  When blighting Winter breathes its icy chill,
And marks with barrenness the dreams of Earth—
  Thine inner joy, to light its spirit still !

GREAT TEMPLE OF KARNAK.

Thou art not now ; a far-off age did knell
A greater death, that marked thy lesser fall,
Thou mighty temple, reared by Egypt's thrall !
What grandeur do thy silent ruins tell,
Wherein a thousand buried arts do dwell !
O Karnak ! wondrous e'en thy mould'ring wall,
Whose countless crumbling monuments recall
The mystic splendor of thine ancient spell !
But wherefore name thy praise ! Forever more,
As ever, thou art dead. Thou ne'er didst live,
Save in the mockery of Truth, to score
The spoils of false, despotic kings ; to give
The tyrant's lash to cringing slave, or fame
To glory, or to baser gods a name !

THE FALLEN SHAFT.

UNDER EAGLE CLIFF, LAKE MOHONK.

About thy base its giant fragments lie.
What power, what silence ; mighty solitude !
Through age on age, in towering grandeur, stood
The broken, balanced shaft against the sky,
Riven from thy battlement of rock on high.
The glaciers once crushed through thy wild abode,
The Titan thunders oft thy summit rode.
These, it withstood, their ruin to defy ;
But, ah ! thou subtle, sluggish dreamer, Time,—
Stealthy of hand, mute-voiced, unpassioned, thou,—
With patience, through a thousand years, didst steal
Its flinty feet, with aid of rust and clime,
Didst bend its massive form and hoary brow,
And force, at last, the awful wreck to reel.

A VOICE FROM THE SEA.

Once, by the moon-lit sea we stood,
   And watched the shield of glimmering light
That fell across the throbbing flood,
   Melting the shadowy folds of night.

Far o'er the shifting, silvery sand,
   That every rolling wave re-swept,
We heard the billows lave the strand,
   In monody that never slept ;

And far along the sheeny deep,
   We saw the flying fleet of sail
That cleft the swell, and seemed to leap,
   And scorn the threat of gathering gale.

And ah ! the sounds that softly broke
   In ceaseless surges from the sea,
Blent with a murmuring voice, that woke,
   To breathe an answer back to me :

For there beneath the bending sky,—
   Sweet vision of a day that's dead—
One whispered words that ne'er can die,
   Whose earthly image long since fled.

Break thou, O purple waves, for aye,
   And lade the winds, and kiss the shore,
For, all in vain, I dream a day
   Shall bring me back that voice of yore.

Yet, yet, along the strand, alone,
   I watch the never-dying sea,
And hear the never-dying tone
   From lips that whispered love to me!

A JUNE SONG.

A heart in the June-day of Summer
   Had tasted the violet's lips;—
Had stolen from every new-comer
   The honey that lover-heart sips;
Had traversed the low-lands, the high-lands,
   To drink of the dewy sweets there;
Had wandered through near-lands and far-lands
   The blossoms of Summer to share;

Till, longing and lonely,—a-sighing
   For love of a love that was vain,
For a bliss that ever was dying,
   For a joy that covered a pain,—
It winged its far flight over mountain,
   It spanned the purple sea-plain,
It sped to the lily-brimmed fountain
   Of the passion of Youth again;

It listened for a murmur, a laughter,
  It dreamt of a fairy face there,
It pled for an answer, once softer
  Than songs on the Summer-sea air ;
But the voice was hushed in the gloaming,
  The form and the spirit were gone,
The face in the mirror-font foaming
  Had melted to mist with the morn !

The June-day of Summer was over,
  The Autumn had withered the May,
The bloom of the heart of the lover
  Had faded forever away !

HAUNTED.

In a dim-lit radiance,
  Satin-draped, and marble room,
Palace-walled magnificence,
  Splendor glittering through the gloom,
    Dreamily
Sat a man of fortune favored,
    Musing dreamily.

Time had touched, with chilling frost,
  Heart and life, and blurred their grace
With its gold and bill of cost,
  Robbed of love his soul and face—

Love's fair art—
Love, the child of faith and feeling,
Dead within his heart.

Yet, to-day, he, dreamily,
  Borne on Fancy's idle wing,
Wandered back, in memory,
  Listened to the song of Spring,
    Maiden sung,
Song of truth to heart of lover,
    Ah, when he was young!

And a face, it startled him;
  Worn with grief's unwritten years;
Pale and patient, through the dim,
  Undrawn veil of time and tears;
    Startled him!
Hapless face of love and sorrow,
    Through the shadows, dim.

Never had he seen that face
  Since they parted, long ago;
Since the broken vow—the place
  Where she dwelt, he did not know,
    But to-day,
Idle fancy,—cursèd dreamer—
    Led him all the way;

And her eyes upbraided him,
  Passionless, unpleading now,

Looking, looking, not for him,
  Since the faithless, broken vow,
    Haunting eyes,
Love's deep embers,—dying embers—
  Lost in wild surprise.

Still her face, unveiled to him,
  Seen through Time's relentless guise,
Haunted, aye, it haunted him,
  Seared him with its burning eyes—
    Tearless eyes—
Ever looking through the shadows,
  Worlds of sad surprise.

" 'TWAS YEARS AGO."

I.

'Twas years ago, my love, that we
  Within an old home-forest stood,
And plighted hearts, and dearly wooed,
  And cut our names upon a tree ;
Dost thou recall ? May's violets fair,
And sweet arbutus wreathed thy hair ;
  The shadow and the gold-lit ray,
  Together danced across our way ;
Beneath the dome of blue-built sky,
  The lofty wood, the virgin green,

Bent o'er us like a mantle high,
   And made for us a welcome screen.

II.

Once more—full twenty years have gone—
   O Love, we wander hand in hand
Here, on a fair mid-summer morn,
   Beneath the shade of that home land;
The names have sunken in the tree,
   Yet, true to its sweet trust, it keeps,
   Sacred within these lonely deeps,
Their meaning clear to thee and me;
   And do they tell thy love as when
   We carved them in the May time then,
   With May's arbutus in thy hair,
   And May's fresh violets in thy hair?

ON THE BANKS OF THE SOUHEGAN.

The summer air is sweet with balm,
   The river like a mirror lies,
Reflecting back the tranquil calm
   Of Hampshire's golden sunset skies;

The waters murmur on the same,
   Their melodies of ages long;
The hills, so often called by name,
   Still answer back the voice of song.

The forest trail, that, in the days
   Of youth I roamed, the sinuous stream
Along whose marge, by devious ways,
   I wandered in my earlier dream ;

And all the slumberous solitude
   Within the old familiar glen,
Are as they were of yore, and brood
   Within my spirit now as then.

I hear the sylvan voices break
   Far in the deeps of birch and pine,
Where summer's wingèd songsters wake
   To thrill again with notes divine.

I stroll along the pebbly strand,
   Or wander o'er the drowsy steep ;
The meadow, lake, and slope expand
   In hazy harmonies of sleep.

And on the grassy ledge I lie,
   Unmindful of the world beyond,
Linked to the heart of memory,
   And sweetly cherishing the bond.

I close my eyes, and up the stream
   Of life return, in fancy dear,
To those fair days of youth and dream
   When oft I rowed the river here ;

Until, oblivious of the years,
    Afar through mists of world and time,
A phantom boatman steers and veers
    His barque, like music in a rhyme.

His form is lithe, his eye is keen,
    His song keeps time to dipping oars;
He sings with heart and faith serene,
    And leaves behind the merging shores

He leaves behind the hedge and ferns,
    The sheltering trees and mimic slopes,
As in his soul a passion burns
    That stirs his life with larger hopes.

His homely craft recoils and shifts,
    Where deeper currents speed him on,
Then down the broadening waters drifts,
    And rounds the point and he is gone.

And he is gone for aye and aye;
    He never more as boy returns,
But now, in sober manhood's day,
    He plucks again the river ferns.

A sterner world of stress and pain,
    A world of love, and thought, and strife,
Of storm and calm, of loss and gain,
    Has knit his heart to other life.

Yet here, in Memory's sweet repose,
   Where once his halcyon hopes were born,
He sings his song of these, for those
   Who then were here, but now are gone.

THE DEATH-ROLL OF HONOR.[2]

No muffled drum beats o'er the grave,
   No shattered columns tell the story,
Not one survives, of all the brave,
   To wear the crown of glory.

No message from the leader's hand;
   He wrote his last with sabre gleaming;
Then fell amidst his deathless band,
   A soldier's vow redeeming.

What desperate honor there was won!
   Alas! no hero lives to name it;
Yet Spartan mother, for her son,
   Might clasp his shield to claim it!

Bring purest marble from its tomb,
   Unquarried through the nameless ages;
And, grave this last, from History's loom,
   On its fair, polished pages.

Such courage burns anew in death ;
  By it fresh altar-fires are litten ;
And in its quickening, fiery breath,
  Fresh honor-rolls are written.

JUST BEYOND.

Through the forests I have strayed,
  Over upland steeps have climbed,
Traversed tracks where sun and shade
  With a silent music rhymed,
Through the lowly vales have passed,
  Followed under cliff and crest,
Scaled the heights of summits vast,
  Mounted to the eagle's nest ;
Touched, a moment, at the goal
  Which, ere reached, seemed paradise ;
Then it vanished from my soul !
  Then it faded from my eyes !

Now a wandering dream I've chased—
  Idlewild, or strange romance ;
Now my days have gone to waste,
  Foiled by frowning circumstance ;
Now a glimpse from cross to crown,
  Now a visionary heaven,

Now a treasured world unknown,
  Fancy to my thought has given.
Still with restless, anxious heart,
  Or with heedless, careless glee,
I have dwelt from men apart,
  On the land and on the sea,

Seeking that I could not find,
  Longing for the unattained,
Straining eyes that yet were blind
  To the marvels never gained ;
Followed, lured by many a form,
  Hidden paths, through gloom and night ;
Battled passion, pain, and storm ;
  Prayed for calm and peace and light ;
Onward, onward, onward still,
  Led o'er nameless shining ways,
I have searched, with tireless will,
  For the crown of earth and days.

It is mine ; yet never can
  Hand or heart possess it all ;
Ever will it lead the van
  Just beyond my ken and call.
I shall see its beckoning fire
  Upward through the shadows peer,
Follow it from height to higher,
  Now afar and now anear ;

But, alas! may never know,
   Nor, with mortal sense or sight,
Win the prize I covet so,
   With its calm of peace and light!

CONTRASTED.

I knew them both, and could but own
   That both were fair and true;
But, ah, how different in tone—
   How wide apart they grew!

In that blue eye, and plain address,
   One scarcely saw, yet felt,
What energy of gentleness,
   And quiet purpose dwelt.

Her speech, with unaffectedness,
   Lit up her modest face;
And beauty marked her none the less
   For her unconscious grace.

She loved the noble virtues best,
   And felt a silent dread—
Not all concealed, yet unexpressed,
   For spirits meanly bred.

And many a heart, when lowly bent,
   And tempted to despair,
Has felt that her sweet presence, meant
   An answer to its prayer.

Not passionless, or soulless born;
   Yet shallow beings lost
The deepness of her life, that shone
   Through sacrifice and cost.

Then, on the other face I mused,
   Of a far different mould,
Of peerless beauty—not unused
   To have its graces told.

Her eyes were bright with fitful light,
   Or armed with scornful glance;
Her words were lavish of delight,
   Or heedless speech perchance.

She plucked the gorgeous colored flowers,
   She loved the buoyant throng;
And even, through the anxious hours,
   She sang a laughing song.

You'd call her heartless? Could you know
   The secret of her thought,
The hidden tears, the passion's glow,
   The purpose yet unwrought,

You would not lightly hold her worth,
    Nor pass her in disdain ;
A spirit, giving out its mirth,
    Will often hide a pain.

And I, who knew them, dare aver
    That both were fair and true.
Yet, ah, how different they were,
    How wide apart they grew !

TWO RIVERS.

I.

Two rivers to the sea are bound,—
    The one a murmur through the vale ;
Eddies and laughter—nymphs of sound—
    Dance and die in its wilderness trail ;
On through the wold, the waste, the glen,
    Glad to escape the bickering throng,
Borne through solitude, heedless of men,
    It sings forever its virgin song.

Over its silvery, sandy brink
    The ferns and filmy mosses grow ;
Daisies, wild, on its borders prink,
    And gold and purple blow and glow ;

Choired in the emerald heights above,
  Sing, with the music of the breeze.
Birds from the tropical lands of love,
  Sighs from the far Hesperides.

II.

Two rivers to the sea are bound,—
  The other, vast, and broad, and deep,
Whose surges bear incessant sound
  Of music from the hills of sleep;
Whenever the tempests sweep its sides
  It frowns defiance in its waves,
Whose billows leap in mighty tides,
  Or moan in their mammoth caves.

Ebbing and flowing, never at rest,
  It bears its freight from main to main,
Angered by every stormy crest,
  Calm with calm of heaven again;
Mindless of man, forever it goes,
  On and on, to the sea, to the sea,
Father of all the land bestows,
  Child of ocean's eternity.

III.

To the world the poet brings his boon,
  From haunts of the silent sylvan wood,
From dreams of the shadowy noon and moon,
  From the deeps of Nature's solitude;

His notes are tuned in a lonely strain,
  To the voice and heart of harmony,
Yet to men, alas! the song is vain,
  'Tis born in the germ of Liberty.

Then a master song the poet sings,—
  It swells to the ebb and flow of tides,
Strong and deep are its minstrelings
  As down to the sea its music glides.
It floods, and floods the land again,
  With its voice and heart of harmony,
Yet to men, alas! the song is vain,
  'Tis born in the faith of Liberty.

A FRIEND.

The memory of a cherished friend,
  The thoughts that cluster round his name,
Are blessèd lights that fondly lend
  A lustre lost to common fame.

To tell the genius of his mind,
  The beauty of his noble face,
The heart that held it only kind
  To exercise each higher grace;

To guard as precious relics now,
  And oft, with faltering voice, relate

The sacred pledge, the mutual vow
  That death alone could dissipate.

These bind the lips to service dear,
  And free the pulses of the heart,
Till fancy, dreaming he is near,
  Reclaims him by its matchless art.

In him the gentler virtues blent,
  With dignity of Nature's mould ;
Alike his kindly spirit bent
  To Summer's cheer or Winter's cold.

His charity was ever large,
  A student of the higher laws—
He held it sacred to discharge
  The broadest service to the cause.

He builded wider than the creeds,
  Nor cared his own should be defined :
His gospel wrote itself in deeds
  And kept its faith in humankind.

MARCH.

Mists inveil the earth and sky;
   Tempests shake their angry sleets,
Fierce with ominous lullaby,
   O'er the dreary, dismal streets.

Desolate, forbidding days,
   Born of Winter's dying breath,
Deluge now the lowly ways,
   From her melting ghosts of death.

Voices, phantoms from the haunts,
   From the caverns and the keeps
Of dumb Nature's hollow wants,
   Echo from her barren steeps.

Wailing winds, in mournful tone,
   Unavailing, tell their pain,
As if searching for their own,
   O'er the fields of Winter-slain.

Yet thou art the month of tears,
   Broken-hearted, and we find,
Through the ever-forming years,
   That thy sullen clouds are lined,—

That behind thy brusque disguise
   Kindness lurks, and golden haze,
Breathing Nature's softest sighs,
   Weaving there her violet Mays.

Ah ! thou heart of wild complaint,
   Mute regrets, and hopeless pain,
Stay, ere utterly thou faint,
   Life and Love will come again !

FARE YE WELL.

" I am going home," she said,
" Ere the Autumn leaves are shed."
And the gold and crimson glow
Of the setting sun, burned low,
Through her curtained casement, red.
" I am going home," she said,
" To the silence of the dead.

" Death, O shadow, thou, of life,
Strife that triumphs over strife,
Pain that masters meaner pain,
Gain, from loss of lesser gain,
Life that's born of life that's dead,
Ghost of years forever fled,
I shall know thee soon," she said.

"I am going where the light
Never fades away to night,
Where the loss of earth and sense,
Finds ethereal recompense,
Where the heart of love and truth,
Victor over orphaned ruth—
Burns with a perpetual youth.

"I am going," and her lips
Faltered, as her finger-tips
Pressed a lingering adieu ;
And her eyes of heavenly blue
Longing, looked, as if to say,
" Fare ye well, I pass away
To the realms of endless day.
   Fare ye well ! "

DEATH.

Thou canst not frown, O Death ! Thy sullen brow
Is marble-cast ; thine ear is deaf and dead
To sound ; thine eyes are blind, and thou art led
By wandering Chance, nor knowest where, or how ;
Nor smile nor frown can move thy visage now,
To fill the cup of joy or pain. 'Tis said
Thou hast no touch of sorrow for the bed
Of anguish ; thou dost scorn both weal and woe,

And, merciless and pitiless, dost change
The purposes of men with frosted breath ;
Dost snap sweet ties and gentle bonds of love,
And in thy prison-house—the grave—with strange,
Relentless hand, dost bind the soul, O Death,
And cheat the spirit of its home above.

FAITH.

Yet, Death, thou art not victor. Through the gloom
Of thy veiled face, like some dim-visioned height
In shadow, dawns the spirit's quenchless light,—
The vast reality of love,—to loom
Beyond the shuddering silence of the tomb !
O Christly Faith, but lift, in gentle might,
The standard of thy Master, and the night
Doth melt in day, sublimer thought doth bloom
And flower, and holier laws compel the heart,
Till, uncompelled, all souls, made true as free,
Shall hear, enwrapped, the voiceless, heavenly choirs,
In unimagined glorias, impart
The perfect song of immortality,
The full fruition of divine desires.

MATINS.

Sleep from my eyes had fled : Silence and Night,
Two gloomy spirits, gave to solitude
A double shade, until its darkling mood
Had filled my mind with tremulous gleams of light,
As, when a veil enfolds the human sight,
The busy brain is quickened by a flood
Of dreams, so Fancy conjured up her brood,
That put all sober worlds of thought to flight ;
And sleepless, and with vivid ear I lay,
When, breathless, and from out the stillness shot
A clear and liquid voice, an arrowy ray
Of thrilling music, like a sudden thought :
I listened, and again from quivering throat,
O welcome song, the early robin's note !

"THE CHOIR INVISIBLE."

Sweet minstrelsy, that holds, and ever will,
Dominion over men, thou wert not born
Alone in visions of earth's early morn,
Ere wisdom clipped their wingèd dreams, to fill
With deepening lore the classic page, for still,
E'en though the gods are lost, and grope forlorn,
Heaven's angels brood wherever faith is borne
In beatific prayer and song, to thrill
The soul with imagery divine.

                        O, teach
Thou ever, Truth, (God's messenger) of light
And love enwrapt, and angel-winged, nor may
The dull philosophies of men outreach
The glory of transfigured thought, whose sight,
Prophetic, touches immortality.

A SERENADE.

When the mid-moon is hung in heaven,
    When the stars are studding space,
And a motionless beauty is given
    To Night, in its myriad face,
When, hushed, like a whispered answer,
    The sheen of the silver sea
Reflects the circling censer,
    In its journey of light, for me:

O Love, then I haste to thy meeting;
    I breathe, in the scent of night
And the rose, the joy of thy greeting,
    Like the song of bird in flight,
Like a voice from the stilly spaces,
    Thy voice I hear, and I see
Thy form as a vision, with graces
    My fancy has imaged to me.

To the light in the vale, in thy casement,
    (Ah, night, that woos me to mine,
Deem not that thy darkling effacement
    Can dim my spirit in thine!)
To thee, Love, awaiting my calling,
    I am borne on wingèd feet,

Where the vaporous dews are falling,
  Where day-throbs have ceased to beat.

I list to the musical silence,
  I touch the tremulous strings,
Till the fire that quickens from thy glance,
  Inspires my minstrelings ;
Disdain not, O Vision, if thou art,
  Or form of Beauty, divine,
To linger, to listen, would'st know not
  The love, the heart that is thine?

Not soft words the bosom may sigh for,
  Plead I of thy lips, to-night,
Nor the spell, the passions that die, or
  The fervor that faints in light,
But a love that never may falter,
  A joy that never can flee,
Thine innermost being whose altar
  Within my being shall be.

Now, over the limitless ocean,
  Away on the tide of life,
Where the heart may dream thy devotion
  When thought has sickened of strife,
I go ; and a troth, aye, a promise,
  From one who alone can be mine,
Give thou, and wherever thy home is,
  My spirit shall mingle with thine.

THE SECRET.

"I cannot sing, my heart is faint, and love, like some dead burden, lies
Across my bosom; yet no plaint my lips may breathe, or broken sighs;
For life, alas, has come to be a sad and reverent thing to me.

"I know, I know the world is wide, and every breast must bear its own
Of misery, and hearts must hide their secrets deep, and live alone:
Yet, dear one, aye, and more than friend, a few short moments thou wilt lend?

"Come, Sweet, and in the wooded deeps, on yonder mossy bank, awhile
The burning sun its glory keeps, we'll sit and watch its lingering smile;
Thy hand in mine, thine arm to brace me, while I look into thy face—

"As in the autumns gone would he, with burning speech and strong embrace,
Draw close a folding arm round me, and gaze, so deeply, in my face,

To tell his love ; his voice would thrill me so, that
memory hears it still.

" I cannot brook the thought ; e'en now it sways
me spite of scornful tears ;
How could lips mock in such a vow, to crush
through agony of years,
Or tell their empty words, to make the heart to
trust, and then to break ?

" Dear friend, alas, in those fair days, (it seems
an age since they were born,)
We gathered in the purple Mays, fresh wreaths
that years ago were worn ;
Ah me, sweet life of promise given, so soon to lose
its touch of heaven !

" For Love is heaven's brightest star, the sun of
every glorious thing ;
Without it, joy must live afar, and hope can bring
no offering ;
Without it, thought is but a pain ; the heart within
itself is slain !

" And O, my friend, our love was true ; up through
the glades we used to wind,
And there, for kiss his lips would sue, with ardent
words, and undesigned,
And many a twilight found us, still unheeding, on
the distant hill ;

"Then, he was never false I know; we talked
 beneath the chestnut boughs,
And built our castles; soft and low the breezes
 bore our equal vows;
We listened to the robin sing, and answered on as
 light a wing;

"You know it all,—the same sad truth,—and think
 lost souls like his, must pay
The forfeit due to nobler youth, for garlands woven
 in the May?
Well, be it so, and yet, and yet, what solace this for
 vain regret?

"For vain regret! O, when the life, heart-broken
 all, deserted, lies
At foot of some o'erconquering strife, when Love
 unexpiated, dies,
And Grief, impatient, waits the end, with only one
 to claim as friend!

"Forgive, dear heart, I know that tears from thy
 sweet eyes are deeply wrung;
Thou need'st not deem my woes are fears, dull Fear
 was shed when I was young;
My heart has all its courage still, and ills! there is
 no other ill;

"Could I but deftly dream it off, this world of
 unimagined pain,

By some narcotic, sleep or laugh the banished
    heart's-ease back again,
How light, then, were love's bonds, to wear or cast
    aside, without a care!

" This sorrow colors all my thought; it deepens to
    the soul of things;
The senses are with spirit fraught, and nature feeds
    on hidden springs;
A heart is in the flower, that pleads as if it knew
    my inmost needs!

" I hear the softer breezes sigh and languish, play-
    ing their light notes
As mindful that they, too, must die, e'en while
    their minor music floats;
The brooklet, in its lone retreat, seems oft to rest
    its rhythmic feet.

" And I am come, at last, so near the ghostly
    shadow, that I feel
Its touch, and know its hand; the dear soft amber
    sunsets but reveal,
In gathering pathos from the west, the sinking of
    my life to rest.

" The rustling of the autumn leaves, the moaning
    of the autumn wind,
The clusters of yon banded sheaves, are ever bring-
    ing to my mind

That life is but a fleeting dream, fast dying like the
    sunset's gleam.

" For love is life to me, and O, the loss of love is life
    no more !
I murmur not, death is no foe, its dread with me
    has lost its power,
And yet, I would that one should know my hidden,
    secret world of woe.

" I tell thee all ; for other ears my lips have worn a
    sacred seal ;
To others, mine were idle tears ; for me, no other
    friends could feel ;
I tell thee all ; and wilt thou share the thoughts I
    could no longer bear ?

" And should he come when I am gone, tell him
    that I forgive the pain,
Tell him I bore it all alone—my cross—dear Christ,
    it has its gain,
For it has taught my heart its shrine, and made
    life's common ways divine ! "

She paused ; the sun, with after-glow of glory,
    tinged the slanting west ;
The waters, from their distant flow, in cadenced
    ripples, sang of rest ;
The whippoorwill, from the dusky sky, ominous,
    sent forth its lonely cry.

She heard the chorus of the night intone the
    autumn of the year ;
She gazed forth on the dimming light with eyes too
    sad for hope or tear ;
And felt, low brooding overhead, the waiting angel
    of the dead.

UNINTERPRETED.

Within the vale-embosomed wold,
    Low droop the tasselled chestnut boughs;
    Soft lullabies of sweet repose
Still murmur, as in days of old.

Deep in the sleeping solitude,
    Half-muffled in its ferny dream,
    The silver ripple of the stream
Whispers its ancient interlude ;

While, far aloft, the busy wren,
    Or thrush, or lark, in luteful strain,
    Flings wild its pang of joy or pain,
In echoes, through the hollow glen.

And here awhile I muse in thought,
    How, through the countless eons gone,
    The circling birds have sang alone,
In language man was never taught.

UNINTERPRETED.

Thick sheltered from the common way,
   Who knows what airy spirit thrills
   The feathered throat, what rapture fills,
Or tender vows inspire its lay?

Who knows the lyrical caress,—
   An art by man scarce understood,—
   By which the birdling's heart is wooed
To Love's delirium of bliss?

Who knows the sadness that it sings?
   Its chidings to its lover-mate?
   Or fond reply, or scornful hate
Marked in the flutter of its wings?—

What sighs intone its music so?
   What passions tremble in its song?
   What questionings of right or wrong
Impel its answer, "Yes" or "No"?

What code of wisdom teaches it?
   What yearnings fill its aching breast?
   What glory of celestial rest,
Eternal, in its soul is lit?

Who knows, ah! who? We can but guess
   An inly answer, as we sing,
   Or think, a vain imagining,
But all without is nothingness.

Yet, might I know,—or foul, or fair,
   Whatever fortune wins the day,—
That birds would fill my wandering way
With their wild songs—I would not care.

OLD HUNDRED.
1776-1876.

The nation's agèd Century sat
   Alone ; the cold chills crept within
His veins ; his shrivelled form, once fat
   And round, had shrunk to bone and skin.

His mind was tenantless of thought ;
   His friends, who once had served him true,
Had—one by one—departing, sought
   The promised favors of the new.

A hundred years had crowned with frost,
   His hollow temples ; while the blows
Of countless battles, won and lost,
   With treacherous friends and noble foes,

Were stamped upon his ancient breast,
   Whose glories soon would fade in gloom ;
Their noisy echoes sink to rest
   In history's dim ancestral tomb.

His wasted features, grim and gaunt,
   Like frightful crags and caverns, frowned
On every sight. Not hungry want,
   But yet, some brooding fate, had bound

In withering grasp his wrinkled face ;
   Had lit with vacant stare his eye.
'Twas plain the old man's earthly race
   Was run, and he was doomed to die.

The candle to the socket spent,
   Now flickering, gasped its feeble breath ;
While spectral shadows came and went,
   Like phantom images of death.

The fire had deadened on his hearth,
   The embers shed a pallid glow ;
Like refuse from the after-math,
   The ashes lay in heaps below.

Adown the dingy chimney-flue,
   The bass-voiced tempest sounded near,
And blent with shriller winds that blew
   Their wailings to the old man's ear.

He heard them not, till, from afar,
   There came the crash of mighty sounds ;
The very heavens seemed to jar,
   The earth to wheel in swifter rounds.

Ten thousand bells peal through the sky !
Ten thousand thund'ring cannon roar !
What means yon wildly swelling cry,
   That echoes back from mount to shore ?

Once more the Centenarian starts ;
   Through every quiv'ring nerve and limb
He feels the deadly pang that darts ;
   His tottering feet fail under him.

Once more his eye peers through the night,
   Through which a lightning flash is shed ;
A new-born Century looms in sight !
   Old man ? *Old man?* He's stark and dead !

PARNASSUS.

WILLIAM CULLEN BRYANT.

OBIIT, JUNE 12, 1878.

A maiden's song to the mountain air
Was carolled along from height to height,
A minstrel of love on its musical flight,
To free the heart from its lonely lair ;
It led it astray, like a child at play,
It wove it a dream by a forest stream,
Like a bird on the wing to its tropical spring,
From its nest on the crest of the mountain.

The song was wafted afar and away—
A faintly murmuring undertone—
Till through the woods it wandered alone.
It rivalled the brook in its roundelay;
It sped from the glen to the haunts of men,
And touched the spirit of those who would hear it,
And it melted to song the din of the throng,—
This lone siren-voice from the mountain.

The fern and the flower were in the song,
The heart of the plaintive pine was sighing
With winds that on dizzy cliffs were dying,
And the odors of summer were borne along
With sylvan loves laden. The song of the maiden
Was, "Come to the mountain, to its cool, mossy fountain,
From city and sea, O, come and be free!
On the hoary-crowned heights of the mountain."

Then the weary-worn waifs from sickly climes,
The slaves from the dingy delves of earth,
The foolish fairies of fashion and mirth,
Caught up the mountain-maiden's rhymes,
And spreading wings for the heavenly springs,
They floated away on the mystic lay,
Where sunlight is born, in the golden morn,
To the skyey peaks of the mountain.

Alas! in vain, by caverns and ledges,
The wanderers followed the luring note

Of the song they heard, so far remote,
From the fair maid's lips ; 'neath rifts and ridges
They chased the gleam of the forest stream,
They hearkened again for the murmurous strain,
But it died away like the dying day,
In the fasts of the trackless mountain.

One only, whose spirit was steeped in light,
A poet who strayed from the motley throng,
Drank deep of the maiden's matchless song,
As it echoed from a shadowy height ;
And he followed the theme through many a dream,
That led him afar by the light of a star,
'Neath a lofty crest to the maiden's rest,
By the fall of a virginal fountain.

And he wooed the maiden with her native dower ;
While he rhymed of forest and mossy cave,
Till his heart was full of the love she gave ;
And he wove her wreaths of fern and of flower—
With a poet's vow he circled her brow,
For better or worse, in immortal verse,
In the solitude of the mountain.

L'AVENIR.

My ship is launched on the ocean tides,
    With its silver-sail unfurled ;
Its glistening keel over fathoms glides,
    Bound on to the underworld.

It sails to the far Hesperides,
    To magical gardens, where
The gold fruit of the Orient trees
    Gleams in the Orient air.

Its banners wave on the wind-swept sea,
    And I watch its spectral spars
Float down the bending horizon for me,
    Emblazed in the morning bars.

I know it will ride the swelling gale,
    I dream of the mystic days,
When again shall loom its silver-sail
    From out the Orient haze.

A MEDLEY.

I listened to the sounds that burst,
    Half-muffled, on my ear ;
The deep, bass tones growled low at first,
    Now distant, now more clear ;
Then, then tumultuous, they railed
    In hoarse and hollow wrath,
To break in clashing chords that hailed
    Their mock-artillery forth.

In mimicry of shot and shell
    The heavy notes rebounded ;
From wild pathos to dying knell,
    Half human, they resounded ;
They seemed to battle in mid-air,
    They waned to stifled moanings,
As if a desolate despair
    Had hushed their harsh intonings.

Still higher up the scale they scored
    A hundred minuets,
They drummed across the sounding-board,
    And rained their treble jets ;
They rippled like the scurrying brook
    Along its pebbly bed,

Then soared aloft, and thrilled and shook
  Like bird-songs overhead.

How deftly now key answered key
  In skips and somersaults;
They stirred the air with melody,
  They came to sudden halts;
They stormed, they laughed, they cried again,
  They pled a piteous tale,
They languished, as in utter pain,
  Along the minor scale.

Then softer, sadder, sweeter still,
  Their music blent with themes
That soothed my aching sense, to thrill
  My heart with haunting dreams;
A song, aye, like a far-off bell,
  An olden song I heard;
O'er stringless harps it wrought its spell,
  With neither sound or word.

FLOOD TIDE.

The flooding tide is drifting o'er the sand;
    It sweeps far up beyond the ocean's edge,
To bear its foamy crest along the strand
    In thundering laughters to the rocky ledge.

What throbbings stir the sea from inward deeps,
    That all the world is girded with its song?
What life from some perennial fountain keeps
    Its billows rolling through the ages long?

When years were few and fair within my breast,
    I did not question thus, for then I felt
The same wild flood of life, of glad unrest,
    From the full fountain that within me dwelt.

But hark! the sea is calm and peaceful now;
    The noon has stilled its giant waves,—it lies
Serene, reflecting back the bending brow
    Of heaven, the cloud and purple of its skies.

Ah, Life! thy noon hath touched my pulse, and lo!
    Its vexing tumults for a moment cease;
The flooding tide has had its noisy flow,
    And, ebbing, soon will murmur its decrease.

O Sea! O Life! whose passioned youth is gone,
   Since thou must wane ere yet the day is dead,
Bear to some other golden-freighted morn
   Thy swelling tide, its happy shore to wed :

Yet let thy music through the memory sound,
   With soft receding echoes from the past,
Until I hear thy circling tides rebound,
   Bringing with them immortal youth at last !

AH, COULD WE KNOW!

We, waiting, watched beside her bed,
And thought a nimbus crowned her head,
As lying there, the calm face seemed
An angel's from the earth redeemed.

Full seventy years her patient love
Had mixed with life, to nobly prove
The Master's spirit in her own,
That seemed to live so near his throne.

We hoped, alas, her ill might stay
Its mortal plague, and that the May
Would touch her with its sunnier breath,
To dissipate the Shadow, Death.

And o'er our mother's form we bent ;
Our hearts in passioned bosoms pent ;
The house itself was blank and dumb,
Prophetic of the grief to come.

Our sister held her feeble arm,
To feel the pulse's faint alarm,
And at a whisper, raised her head,
"To ease and comfort her," she said.

We watched the ominous change that fell
Across her features—Death's mute knell—
And gazed with weeping, trancèd eyes,
As if to see her spirit rise.

Sweet face, deep furrowed, suffering face,
So hallowed of Immanuel grace !
A grace that death had never given,
Made beauteous in the peace of Heaven.

We could not see behind the veil
Of that still shadow, lifeless pale ;
Our prayers, our tears in vain were spent,
Our utmost souls were impotent.

Ah, could we know the realm, afar,
To what dear planet, what blest star,
Her being took the homeward flight,
What love would sanctify its light !

IN EMBRYO.

When Nature opes her doors to spring-time days,
    And gentle maidens murmur fresh-made songs ;
When purple May-flowers spring in untrod ways,
    And every half-fledged youth, impassioned, longs

For Love's warm heart to burst its petals sweet,
    To hold its rose-lips up for kisses fair,
With little thought to bear itself discreet,
    But, generous to bestow a lavish share ;

O, when the rills from winter's bondage free,
    Fill all the valley-wood with victory's cheer,
And answer trill for trill with earliest glee
    Of some gay songster from the olden year,—

Then thrill my pulses with a wanton joy,
    As if a thousand new-created veins
In me had filled with nectar-wine, to buoy
    The lagging blood ; then thought, up-welling, strains

To leap the verge of sense ; round each light hope
    A golden circle rims ; each joy, foretold,
In memory finds its mate, as shadows grope
    Beside the sun-lit form. O, who can hold

The spirit then, or fetter any thing,
  Of mind or heart, that craves an utterance ?
The tripping fancy, drunk with dewy spring,
  Brings vagrant children to a mart, for once,

Where every wild imagining is clad
  In poet's garb, and set to lyric bars,
Whose trembling harmonies, e'en, make us glad,
  As silvery echoes from the choral stars.

CONTRASTS.

TWILIGHT.

I.

Thy passive hour is often full of deeps ;
  The sun has left its after-glow far east ;
  O Twilight ! thou art stolen beauty ! least
And last of day,—an amber-calm, that keeps
The soul inlit with Heaven, and strangely steeps
  With low imbosomed song (true minstrel feast)
  The fairy imagery of thought ; released
From sterner ways, the dreamy fancy sleeps
  In revery ; the world is hushed, and spirit
    Answers spirit in language of its own,
Without the whisper, or the ear to hear it,
  As one, alone, who is not all alone ;—
And stilly voices echo on the air,
And silent songs melt into silent prayer.

II.

I hear the swift winds sweep along the west,
   Invisible—Heaven's armies put to flight!—
   First far, then near, their giant wings affright
The wailing forest-trees, that vainly breast
Their torrent-force. And yet the sound is rest;
   I love it—fierce, defiant—in its might,
   It lulls, like roar of ocean waves at night;
Companion-like, I love its tumults best;
For I am weak, and strong, and nothing long,
   Fretting against the narrow walls of sense,
Impatient of the unimpassioned throng,
   Half-prisoned by dull fate, but still intense,
With will to conquer and compel—a power
That tempts, and yet eludes me every hour!

THE WAITING CHORDS.

Heedless she strayed from note to note—
   A maid—scarce knowing that she sang;
The dainty accents from her throat
   In undulations lightly rang.

She sang in laughing rhythms sweet;
   A bird of spring was in her voice;
Till, on through measures deft and fleet,
   She caught the ditty of her choice.

THE WAITING CHORDS.

A song of love, in words of fire,
   Now made her breast with passion stir ;
It breathed across her living lyre,
   And thrilled the waiting chords in her.

Uplifted like a quivering dart,
   One moment poised the tones on high,
To tell the language of her heart,
   And swell the pean ere it die.

She smote the keys with will and force,
   Like storm-winds swept the sounds along ;
Her flying fingers in their course,
   Vied with the tumult of her song.

Her eyes flashed with the burning theme ;
   A glow of triumph flushed her cheek ;
No need of words to tell the dream
   Of love her lips would never speak.

When the wild cadence died in air,
   And all the chords to silence fell,
I knew the spirit lurking there—
   The secret that had wrought the spell.

FORESHADOWINGS.

Beneath the twilight's brooding shade
She lingered; 'twas a maid,
Fair-haired and beautiful of mien and eye,
Who lonely, by the limpid pool,
Breathed the sweet burden of a sigh,
And felt the kiss of breezes cool.
Simple she was and womanly;
And if sad thoughts can be
Where innocence and pure love make their home,
I deemed that in her eye were some
Dark rays of sorrow vaguely traced,
Which hope or joy had not effaced.
As when the wayward brooklet thrills
With eddies, then, ere long,
By quiet nook, sighs in deep wells, and stills
Its fitful course of laughing song,
To question, there—or seemingly—
Its virgin passion for the sea,
So did her face betoken, now
The fervor of her vow,
And now a voiceless meaning, half of dread,
A dim foreboding thought to wed
A shadow with her love, what time
The marriage bells should haply chime;

And, ah! the timid glances soft,
That peered so, downfalling,
And flush of cheek that, tell-tale, fain would oft,
Like red'ning blossoms in the spring,
Commingle with the deeper gleams,
And light the sombre of her dreams;—
All these, like soft enchantments, passed
In mute impassioned glows,
Illumining eye and face with thoughts, that cast
A sweet uncertainty. "Who knows,"
I said, "the secret of her heart?"
O love, thou hast a matchless art!

VOICELESS.

We met beside the silvery stream,
   The still moon bathed her form in light;
She seemed a fairy-imaged dream,
   Half mantled in the breath of night.

I felt her slight hand clasped in mine,
   O touch, so tremulous with bliss!
Our swift lips pressed to seal the sign,
   And pledge the troth with kiss for kiss.

The night breeze cooled her temples fair,
   Whose fevered pulses bounded high;

The star-mist lit her flowing hair
  And melted in her azure eye.

We strayed far in the covert dell,
  We stole by stealthy ways, that led
To where the shadows deeper fell,
  And wingèd words were fonder said.

There as we murmured, soft and low,
  The old, old love, forever new,
The fringèd ferns seemed all aglow,
  And crimson blushes drank the dew;

All sounds, all sights were blent in one
  Sweet voice, one all-entrancing face;
My wistful heart, that night, had won
  A being touched with angel-grace.

Long years have vanished; as of yore,
  I wander to the same retreat;
I tread the streamlet's mimic shore,
  Where once were pressed her eager feet;

The still moon lights the lonely glade,
  The night-bird hoots its dismal strain;
The gloom within yon forest shade,
  Will never light with love again!

No voice relieves the solitude;
  No song, save in the memory, dear,

Inspires in me the matchless mood
   That once had thrilled my spirit here !

Alas ! I dream of one whose heart
   Bequeathed to me its deathless love,
Whose nameless graces now impart
   Their heaven-lit radiance from above !

SONGS WITHOUT WORDS.

Ah ! hush thy tremulous voice of song,
   And still the noisy bank of keys ;
Too deep, too deep, the joys that throng,—
   Or griefs,—to cherish such as these.

Why mock with nicely studied rote,
   The stringless harp of other days ?
Thou canst not touch its lightest note,
   Nor strike the chord that Memory plays.

No soft, entrancing art of thine
   Can fill the silence of her voice ;
No lips of thine can answer mine,
   Or bid an aching heart rejoice.

Yet, sometimes thou dost snatch a word,
   A tone, an accent from the past,

An utterance that once was heard—
   A moment's thought,—O could it last!

But suddenly, it faints and dies,
   And all again is new and strange;
No other lips can breathe her sighs,
   Alas! they're lost in Time and Change!

THE HEART OF NATURE.

Ah! it is rest to breathe
The airy spirit of the wood,
To hear the music of its solitude,
   Brooklet and bird, to pluck and wreathe
The virgin flowers, fair sisterhood,
   That summer suns bequeathe.

   Soulless? In nature's deeps
Are the embosomed secrets of the mind;
In her lone grandeur and her gloom, behind
   The ever-restless currents, sleeps,
To wake at touch of kindred heart, a kind
   Beneficence, that keeps—

   Beyond the world's annoy—
A refuge where man craves her loves,
And seeks a wilder freedom, as he roves
   In sweet delight, like any boy;

Or where, as in perplexity, he moves,
  She quickens him with joy.

She (mother of us all)
Spreads her wide wings, and kindly broods
Over his waywardness of differing moods,
  Soothes his vain longings, hears the call
Of his mute voice for harmony, and floods
  Him with her answering thrall.

Not harshly does she chide
When he, bereft of some dear hope,
Pleads her to comfort him ; nor bids him grope
  In loneliness when troubles bide,
Or spirit faints, but strews on every slope,
  Her children beautified.

For every grief a flower
Is blown ; for every prayer there rests
A shadow o'er him ; wittingly she tests
  The soul, and blesses with a power,
Lavish of wealth, that his poor life invests
  With unimagined dower.

Say not, O doubting mind,
That she is dumb, and cold, and dead ;
That from her ancient deities is fled
  Their sceptred sovereignty ; nor find,
In Science, thy divinity instead,
  To her veiled beauty blind.

Love rules in her great heart ;
No other potency can woo
And hold to fealty, as she can do,
Or sweetly sway, by any art,
Such inly sympathy of love, so true,
As she fain would impart.

SANFORD R. GIFFORD.

Stilled is his pulse ; his deft right hand
   Is nerveless, that so oft had played
With the soft tints of Orient-land,
   With the weird dream of sun and shade.

Love-like, he worked in wizard ways :
   From dying halos in the west
He wove an amber with the rays
   That crowned the ocean's surging crest.

Not his the veil of night and death,
   Nor his the tempest's awful strife ;
He caught the smile in nature's breath,
   And touched it with illumined life.

His was the master's touch, and his
   The secret, subtle sense to find

Earth's mutable realities
   Transfigured in the raptured mind.

The alchemy of ether-fire,
   The seven prismatic hues, to him
Were strains from some Eolian lyre,
   Or voicings of some mystic hymn.

Like the true poet, in his thought
   An idyl dawned, and, fancy free,
The visioned revery, inly wrought,
   Shone outward over land and sea;

For, ere the colors knew his art,
   Or had expressed his lightest theme,
He saw them blended in his heart,
   And knew the picture in the dream.

But now, alas! when Nature crowns
   The Autumn with its dying flame,
The mourning world, unfeigning, owns
   The starrèd lustre of his name.

THE BLEST.

Rare moments in the realm of mind,
   God gives to man, in which to live
And gain a victory—undefined—
   Beyond the triumphs earth can give.

Not action only wins the palm,
   Nor that wild energy that drives
The jaded brain to banish calm,
   And think that nothing noble thrives;

That coins life's genius into wealth,
   And holds, perchance, that all is lost,
If, by some guilty doubt or stealth,
   It pauses, questioning the cost;

That delves for gold, that masters space,
   Lays tribute on the sea and land,
So one proud race with kindred race
   May barter treasures hand to hand.

Alas, this lucre of the mind!
   Could man but shun it and be wise,
Or break its fetters, he might find
   Fortunes he does not realize;

Blest fortunes at the heart of time,
   God-given to thought; like sea-girt isles
That dwell apart, whose heavenly clime
   The unblest air of earth defiles.

Ah, murmur not, thou doubting soul;
   Nay, listen to the sibyl-voice
That says, "Thou canst not have the whole,
   Life only gives to thee a choice."

"NOT LESS, BUT MORE."

When youth was borne on tireless wings,
   And hope to hope would beck and call,
   When liquid accents held me thrall,
And music woke from golden strings,

Then eagerly my glad heart beat,
   From sheerest turbulence of joy;
   The world was visioned to the boy
In prophecies of fancy sweet.

No boding cloud would o'er me rise,
   No dumb despair within me pall;
   I heard the happier voices call,
And answered back in wild replies;

Or answered back with laughter low,
   That echoed, through the April sky,
   Like mocking minstrelsy, to die
In laughter's clamorous overflow.

Unheeding, then, my utmost thought,
   So frail, that, like the bloom of May,
   It changed with every changing day;
But now, through furnace-fire 'tis wrought!

And now, the glowing sun is veiled;
   The brooding heart has felt its pain;
   The music yields a fitful strain,
And hope's fair prophecies have paled.

Yet, yet, O world! I deem thy store
   Not less, but more; not false, but true;
   I keep thy promised land in view,
And dream of visions more and more!

ONE, A MAIDEN.

Here, beneath the grasses, lies
   One, a maiden, true and sweet;
Fateful, from the summer skies,
   Fell the Shadow at her feet.

Light fled from her gentle eye,
   Dust was written on her brow;
From her lips the lingering sigh
   Pressed to breathe her final vow.

Ere the flower had filled the bloom—
   Part within the bud as yet,—
Death had sent its heavy doom,
   And her earthly sun was set.

Kindly was her simple heart,
   Plain the beauty of her face,
Yet no nice degree of art
   Could have given a fairer grace.

All her golden duties were
   Linked to others' needs and cares;
And their love she won to her
   By the love she lived for theirs;

By the virtue of a mind
   Taught, of many a rare device,
That the heavenly way to find
   Is to lose in sacrifice.

Flowers were strewn above her head,
   And the bending grasses grew
Greener o'er her silent bed,
   Weeping nightly tears of dew.

Yet methinks that when the spring
   Warms, again, this lonely mound,
Flowers of rarer blossoming
   O'er her breast shall then be found:

Violets for her heart of truth,
   Lilies for a life so pure.
Roses for eternal youth
   And a love that shall endure.

THE SWEET MAY-TIME.

O May! whose wild birds sing to me
   Their maiden songs; whose timid flowers
   Make answer to the April showers;
Whose streams leap toward the summer sea;

Whose azure skies and dreamful woods
   Are yet unveiled by summer mist;
   Whose maidenhood is yet unkissed
By summer's sultry solitudes:

I love thy youth:—'tis the first fire
   That warms the petals of the soul;
   That promises a blossomed whole
To the sweet wish of young Desire.

Not heaped with treasure comest thou,
   Nor with a golden honeymoon
   That brings its full delight so soon,
But only with a lover's vow,—

Only the promise and the spring,
   Only the harbinger that holds
   In many closely fitting folds
The germ of some great offering.

O May! thou hast the love of youth
  Imbosomed in thy spirit, given
  Like some diviner faith of heaven
Betrothed to its eternal truth.

THE FIRST SORROW.

Two loved,—the perfumed spring was new,
  The buds were dreaming into flowers,
  The virgin rain, in trembling showers,
Had jewelled the fair land with dew;
    And joyance spread,
    As moments fled.

Two hearts went Maying—mate with mate,
  The air was bathed in amber light,
  While balmy breezes of the night
Stole secrets pledged in wooings late,
    When lover kneeled—
    When troth was sealed.

Two sang—and minstrel voices blent
  In echo through the scented wood;
  The birds—in sylvan loverhood—
Mimicked the songs their rivals sent,
    O hearts, so true,
    To nuptials new!

THE FIRST SORROW.

The shadows deepened as they passed,
   From darkling branches overhead,
   Until a cypress foliage spread
A gloom that hushed their songs at last,
      And words were brief
      With stifling grief.

Awhile in lonely vales they dwelt,
   Embosomed in a sudden sorrow;
   Nor dreamt of gladness on the morrow,
For brooding on the anguish felt.
      For hearts that rend,
      Are slow to mend.

E'er yet the aching grief had ended,
   Low voices—pent with stricken thought—
   With songs of plaintive meaning fraught—
In soft, subduing tones ascended.
      O reverence deep,
      In holy-keep!

They sang, but ever and anon
   They listened for an answering voice,
   And often would restrain the choice
That beckoned back their angel one.
      O memory dear!
      Forever near!

Two loved,—but sorrow looks on high,
   And adds the incense to the shrine;

A bond less earthly than divine,
Had taught them love could never die,
Till meaner joy
Seemed heaven's alloy.

INFINITO.

Could I but grasp the vision, make it mine,
  In one full masterly embrace possess
The splendor of my dream, its joy enshrine,
  And hold it as some trophy-crown, to bless
With perfect calm and peace the conquest won;
  Or could I clear the mist, and fairly face
The high beatitudes of radiant morn,
  That reach through infinite degrees of space;
What then—ah, what? The heart would sigh for
    more;
The longings of a great unrest would send
Swift-wingèd messengers far on before;
  Such glory undefined could only lend
A depth to height, a sadness to desire,—
  A voice forever calling, "Come up higher."

TO F. A. H.[1]

Dear friend, these faltering rhymes of mine and
 thine,
And these frail songs that scarce can bear the
 weight
Of meaning, that betray only the strait
And narrow sense of some vast theme divine ;
What matter that we write a word or line ?
They 're but the shadows, the faint symbols ; late
And early, like the beggar at the gate,
We long to pass beyond the given sign,
To enter at some regal way, to scale
Parnassian heights of unimagined lore ;
But our weak, limping language can but fail,
And we are left, where oft we were before,
Dreaming a prophecy above the din,
A promise—" Sometime ye may enter in ! "

BETROTHED.

Oft have I seen her when her artless art
Would seem to tell her secret to the eye;
Or, when her breast, o'erburdened with its sigh,
Would press to breathe the language of the heart;
And yet it was her highest joy to part
From friend, or e'en her dearest kin, and hie
To solitudes of Eden-thought, and lie
In wait for finer notes of love; then start,
Like frightened fawn at fancied sound of voice,
To seek a covert, where, again alone,
Secure, she'd dream of him, her plighted choice,
Plead to herself the bliss she dare not own;
At last to end her revery in tears,
Ideals of the long-expectant years!

WEDDED.

Once was her heart a rivulet of song—
A lyric fount of pure, melodious verse—
Through which her fleet emotions would disperse
In fitful, murmuring eddies, all day long;
But now, behold a river clear and strong,
Whose restful waters hold sweet-willed converse
With deeper meditations, or traverse
In rhythms which to double lives belong;
And now I know whatever winds may blow
Or storms may break upon the waters deep
Of that true heart, that from the central flow
Of its great love, their course will surely keep
Along the emerald marge of some fair shore,
Where flowerets bud and blossom evermore!

PRESAGING.

It hung on the wall ; a dying blaze
   Lit it up, from the dying sun ;
I gazed on the face as one might gaze
   On the face of an unknown one.
The twilight-dusk, with its gathering gloom,
   Stole stealthily over the wall ;
I sat alone in the silent room,
   Overspread by the deepening pall.

Then the moonlight filled the shadowy place,
   With the magic of its gleam ;
It cast its rays on the motionless face ;
   I started as from a dream,
For the eyes were charged with a living light,—
   Soft eyes that pleaded with me,
Till I felt their deep mysterious sight
   Presaging the years to be.

Though the face, the eyes, of that night are gone,
   Have faded like phantoms in air,
The years that came revealed to me one
   Who answered the image there.

THE MAID OF ANOTHER MAY.

Through green vales she wanders, by virginal
    streams ;
She muses, and wanders, and drinks the soft balm
That Nature distils in the Spring of its dreams,
    And she borrows the peace of its infinite calm.

She sings, as she wanders, a low plaintive song ;
    Not new, like the snatch of a sauntering maid,
But a song that her bosom has carried so long,
    A grief that her bosom has wearily paid :

    " Birds, I heard thee, in the yew-tree,
        Ere the summer breezes stirred ;
    Then I knew thee ; now I rue thee ;
        Once I carolled like a bird.

    " Heedless I, no vows to bind me,
        Love was a wild world of bliss ;
    Come, I said, O Love, and find me,
        Come and win me with a kiss !

    " So Love came, one radiant morning ;
        O, that day ! Alack for this !
    What cared I to take a warning,
        When Love wooed me with a kiss ?

"Wooed me in the purple May-time,
   Till my heart no more was free,
Wooed me with a careless May-rhyme,
   To a Love that loved not me.

" Love, thou art a phantom only ;
   Voiceless dreamer of my heart ;
I am lonely ! I am lonely !
   O, that Love and I could part !"

Thus ever she sings, and her memory still
   Survives in the song that her sad bosom makes.
Ah, the music of love that forever must thrill
   Through her heart, where only its echo awakes !

A FRAGMENT.

I dared not say farewell, but stood
   A statue, chill, and marble pale ;
   Though my heart would mourn and wail,
Never uttered I a word
      When we parted.

I hear a murmur, on the sand,
   Of whispering waves that lave the shore
   With a message,—" Never more,"—
To me,—from an empty land—
      Broken-hearted !

A SONG.

Say not so, say not so,
   Lest my heart abreaking,
Charge thee with its bitter woe,
Curse thee for thy saying so.

Hear my vow, hear my vow,
   Let thy heart, awaking,
Murmur its sweet answer, low,
As our loves together flow;
     Say not no!

A SONG.

I had quaffed from the fountain's full bowl
   When the sun hung high in its place,—
When the heat of the spring-tide mist stole
   Through fevered throbs into my face.
I had quaffed with lips that were blushing,
   The waters that laughed in their glee,—
The waters that leaped as if gushing
   From the depths of a passionate sea.

A SONG.

When the frost-winds had frozen the earth
    I paused at the bare fountain's side;
I heard not the laughter, the mirth;
    The music of waters had died:
For the breath of a chill November
    Had bound with an icy-locked rim
The fountain I fain would remember,
    That played when I drank at the brim.

I had loved, in the bloom of the May,
    A maiden whose love answered mine;
She would sing the swift moments away
    To Love's own rapt cadence divine;
We drank at the wild overflowing
    That brimmed to the lips,—from the bowl
Of Love,—which our spirits, not knowing,
    Had drawn from the passionate soul.

I have sought for the maiden of spring,
    For the lips that mated with mine;
I have longed for the love she would bring,
    And dreamt of the being divine;
But the passion she pledged, no longer
    Wells up from the deeps of her heart,
For the icy-locked seal is stronger
    Than love, that would melt it apart.

A PARTING SONG.

Not long ago, I listened to the song
  A robin trilled, as, from a covert shade,
Beneath a maple's golden bough, its strong,
  Clear voice broke from the stillness of the glade.

To me, the plaintive notes had drawn their sweets
  From Nature's emblems of the waning year.
A flush of glory and of death entreats
  The heart to nameless longings, which endear

The senses to the mem'ry, as they meet
  This vision of the summer's parting bloom ;
And as the redbreast's wondrous song did greet
  My ear, it seemed a plea to stay the doom.

"The past ! the past ! O for a breath of spring !
  Come back to me, ye loves of youth !" it said ;
"O ! hasten, moments, once again, and bring,
  Bring to my brooding wings the loved ones fled."

A dying pathos blended with its tone,
  As if it knew that never more again
Could be reclaimed the happy seasons gone.
  Its wild impassioned song was sung in vain !

Its tired wings, uplifted, beat the air,
  As, breasting onward toward the southern sky,
Noiseless it soared away, I know not where,
  In softer climes to sing its song,—and die.

CARLYLE.

Death, waiting at the gate of day—
  Dumb master of the laws of Time,
  The Fate of worlds, of lives sublime—
Has led him through its silent way.

His spirit glowed with fire intense,
  Of genius lent, and out of pain,
  By dint of truth, he plucked the gain,—
The faith of richer recompense.

Though all the world disown their signs,
  To him transcendent things were true;
  The thoughts that others dreamed he drew
In grand, illuminated lines.

He breathed the poet's lofty clime—
  His virgin loyalty to law—
  Yet wrote the visions that he saw
Without the poet's verse or rhyme.

Nor deigned to work by rote or rule,
  But held the dainty crafts of men
  As something less than human ken,
That slaved the master to the school.

His life to him was more than art :
  He loved to battle—to be strong ;
  For conscience' sake to press the wrong :
'T was kindred to his royal heart.

And, ah ! he loved the wild laments
  That swept, like winds o'er cliffs, athwart
  The steeps of his own mountain thought,
As native with the elements.

Carlyle, we speak thy name in vain ;
  Its echo answers in the air,
  As voices sound from rock to lair,
And vainly echo back again.

Yet now that Time and Sense have wrought
  Their force within thy mortal frame,
  The glory of thy living name
Shall blazon in thy deeds of thought !

DIVIDED.

The wide sea severs friend from friend;
    The sea of life, of thought, of hope;
It drives their sail to veer and wend,
    Through differing courses, down its slope.

One barque is lured to some fair bay
    Where, dreamily, the seasons glide,
To dally with the lighter spray,
    And bathe in whirls of eddying tide.

One blithely dips in sunny deeps,
    As laughing breezes cross its trail,
And fortune-favored, sheers and leaps,
    Unchallenged by the tardy gale.

Yet, by the darkling tempest swept,
    O'er mountain wave, through wintry sleet,
By sterner fate, a third is kept,
    Forever battling with defeat;

While, on the sea, in surge and calm,
    Another rides, a victor, free,
Who plucks a glory from the storm,
    A triumph for her destiny.

Still, far beyond, dismantled, lies
    The wreck of some belated craft,
Whose master tells, with languid sighs,
    Of seas that swept her fore and aft.

And thus, divided, friend from friend,
    On one vast sea, ah, who can say
The wistful thoughts that heart would send
    To heart across the voiceless way!

THE POET'S SONG.

A poet sang a song, once, from the heart;
    The lines that bore its meaning scarce could bear
The cadence of its spirit, or impart
    Its music, so full-laden with the rare,
Deep melodies of life was every rhyme.
    Sometimes it murmured, in its verse, of days
Steeped in the golden dreams of hope sublime,
    That led him back to rose-embosomed ways,

Where the wild verdure blossomed at his feet,
    And fed his heart with fragrant breath of dawn;
Where life, dilating, stirred with romance sweet,
    That tuned his theme to some fair-visioned morn,
Peopling his dream with fantasies of youth
    Ere yet the sullen shadow's pitiless doom

THE POET'S SONG.

Had ever crossed with pale, prophetic truth
   His radiant path, to sere its native bloom.

Sometimes its sinuous thought would lend a tone
   That lingered like low vespers; when his soul,
Embalmed in revery, and left alone,
   Communed with the still stars, or gathered toll
From brooding vale or sleeping solitude;
   Or else, belike, his inly sense would call
Him back to those impassioned years that wooed
   Love's eager lips to his, in blissful thrall.

Then came, alas, a thought to change the spell;
   His voice would tremble in its under-breath,
As he in fancy heard the muffled bell,—
   The virgin knell that bore th' alarm of death;
His deepening spirit felt a burden now!
   Lo, in his saddened song such notes would creep,
Of such emotioned ecstasy of woe,
   That memory only woke to love and weep.

Then, ruefully, he said: "No more I'll sing
   Of that which was, but cannot be again.
Nay, mine shall be a carol on the wing,
   I'll sing of rapture and forget the pain
That memory cherishes; ah, life shall be
   Intoned to sweet enchantments for the ear;
The present, in its plumèd pageantry,
   Shall thrill my melody with noisy cheer.

"In place of music set to notes of calm,
   Which love, in exile, wakens with a sigh,
I 'll touch with sudden transport every charm
   That paints its blazoned beauty for the eye;
Nature shall lose its lonely depths of power
   To draw away from sense my wandering thought,
The Amaranth-wreath, the pressed leaves of the
     flower,
   All heart-reminders, sentiments inwrought

"Of grief for the departed, hopes unblest,—
   These, with the mystery of the silent tomb,
Its unsolved problem and its boding rest,
   Where drooping willows mourn, and hedges
     gloom,
In me no voice shall find, vain shadows they!
   But heedless of the questionings of the mind,
The gala throng shall hear my heedless lay,
   The wooing world shall wed me to its kind."

"And I will sing of fortunes won, of life
   Crowned with a gilded fame, of burning brain
Throbbing amid the thundering wheels of strife,
   Of pleasure careless of the pangs of pain;
The future is but fate, the past is gone;
   Prayer I will never make, nor silent plea;
Alas, the ills that homeless hearts have borne,
   Why lift the veil—enshrouded let them be.

"Splendors of day, and garish scenes of night,
   Music that drowns the thirsty spirit's cry,
The empty incantations of delight,
   The glittering joys that flourish, fade, and die,—
Fair fugitives of time, whose luring arts,
   Beguiling men, may win the world from toil,—
These revels will I sing, nor torture hearts
   With orphaned memory's fruitless dole and spoil."

So said the poet; then he touched the strings,
   But they were all unstrung, the music mute;
No haunting spirit moved his minstrelings,
   The magic tones were hushed on lip and lute!

AGE.

The ivy weaves its mantle green,
   Over the ancient castle-height;
It hides each crevice with a screen,
   And shields the ruined walls from sight.

No sounds of earth's dull troubles jar
   The dreamy sense that o'er it broods,
Weird echoes, breaking from afar,
   Sleep in its haunted solitudes.

AGE.

The swallow stills its noisy tongue,
   Or tempers its harsh chatterings ;
The linnet sings its daintiest song,
   As round the parapet it wings.

The night-owl keeps its vigil hour
   Above the ragged battlements,
And from the vault of its stone tower
   Sends forth its lonely, long laments.

Here Time has sown the peace of age
   To mingle with the hoary rust ;
Tradition tells of lord and page,
   And consecrates the lore of dust.

O Time, thou healer of all ill,
   Bring to each crumbling life a balm ;
In every agèd breast, fulfil
   The blessing of thine ancient calm.

Let memory charm the world away ;
   Bring music sweet, to failing ears ;
Bring joy to thwart the sad decay,
   And ransom for the dying years.

About each silvered crest of age
   Weave there a crown of honor meet ;
Let peace the pangs of earth assuage,
   And write a victory o'er defeat.

THE DYING DAY.

TO E. S. B.

Its path is in the glowing west,
    Embossed with gold and fringed with light;
It holds a prophecy of rest
    Within its gathering folds of night.

It came on silent, airy wings,
    Emblazoned by a heart of fire,
And led to fresh enchanting springs,
    Through many a maze of sweet desire.

From morn till noon its pinions dipped
    To fen and field, and upland lead,
Where Love 'mid luring blossoms sipped,
    And fancy wooed thee with its gleed.

But ere the mid-sun swept the crest,
    Swift moving up the bending heaven,
Grim clouds sailed forth from out the west,
    And sadness to thy soul was given.

Its vapors dimmed the dazzling morn;
    The glittering coronals of earth

Wore sombre hues, and, inly born,
   The shadows fell upon thy mirth.

And Love, and Joy, and Purpose slept,
   And woke again to better ends;
Thy jaded spirit wed and kept
   The hallowed wisdom sorrow sends.

Now saddened voices sing to thee
   From life, outpouring deeper strains,
And lo ! a richer melody
   Consoles thy heart for all its pains.

The pageantry of life is spent,
   Its gilded banners all are furled;
All stilled the harsher discontent,
   And clanging noises of the world.

And stilled at last, thy vexing snares,
   The dreary dreams of goals unwon ;
And hushed are all thy torturing cares,
   So let their haunting masks begone.

The day is dying ; yet again,
   From the last lustre of its crown,
Take thou its lesson, not in vain
   Its cross has weighed thy spirit down.

And as its lingering lights decline,
  As sink its deepening fires below,
Thy thoughts shall wear the heavenly sign,
  The symbol of its afterglow!

"FORGET-ME-NOTS."

When youth was free and joys were young,
  I went a-Maying many a day,
And oh, what heedless songs were sung
  Far in that dreamy, purple May!

When life was fresh, what careless hands
  Stretched forth to pluck the violets sweet,
To weave in wreaths of queenly bands,
  As pressed the bloom my buoyant feet.

I only knew that flowers were fair,
  I only knew that skies were blue,
For round my heart no lurking care
  Had woven shades of sadder hue.

O May! O youth!—no circling years
  Can lead me back to thee again;
I think of thee through hidden tears,
  Or all my thoughts of thee are vain:

For in each wreath that now I twine,
    Dear memory weaves a faded leaf,
And unseen fingers bring to mine
    " Forget-me-nots " for every sheaf.

"AND GIVE GLAD HEARTS THEIR INNING."

What troops of flowers, in emerald deeps,
    By Summer suns attended !
The purple-eyed, that slyly peeps ;
    The queen magnolia splendid ;
The dainty star, the fairy-bell,
    The sad creightonia paling,
The crowfoot of the mossy dell,
    The maidenhair, low trailing.

And from the trees the dogwood sheds
    Its dazzling snows ; the cherry
Blooms forth in skyey, billowy beds,
    With apple-blossoms merry ;
The royal oak. in purpled brown,
    The coral maple vying,
Now stretch their leafy foils, half blown,
    To woo the breezes, sighing.

The woodbine sends its creepers out
   As if for picket duty ;
The ivy winds its toils about ;
   The trumpet blooms to beauty ;
The lilac floods the air with scents,
   The sweet wisteria mating ;
Awhile the deeper tints intense,
   Within their cells are waiting.

The season weaves its wilds among
   The greens, in glowing passions ;
The carpet of the earth, ere long,
   Reveals its wondrous fashions,
When all the floral shrines, upborne,
   Shall spread their tiny graces,
With blessings for the melting morn
   That lights their dewy faces.

Down in the glen the thrushes call,
   The bluebird thrills its lover,
And round some cranny of the wall
   The busy sparrows hover ;
The oriole skims the crystal streams
   That heedless laugh ; and, yonder,
The redbreast wings its airy dreams,
   Or hides its nestlings under.

Why marvel that the earth is fair,
   That joys, like June flowers, springing—

Full-blossomed—deck the grave of care,
   And give glad hearts their inning?
Why marvel that the world is won
   By beauty such as this is?
I, too, my garland-crowns would don,
   And revel in its blisses!

CLOTHED UPON.

I.

Drearily the bleak winds blow
   O'er the withering slopes to-night;
Summers come, and summers go,
   Borne in autumn's chilly flight;
      Well I know

All things change! Ah, all things change!
   Fleet and mutable, they pass.
Dear eyes, now, may turn to strange,
   Love to scorn, perchance. Alas!
      All things change!

O the golden-gate of youth!
   Soon we pass its portal-morn;
Truth has not the fire of Truth
   When the fire of Youth is gone;
      Age and ruth,

Sorrowing in the autumn gale,
  Sighing in the autumn sun,
Wed, and tell their piteous tale,
  Ere the race of Life is run :
        All things fail !

II.

All things fail ? Nay, cease thy plaint ;
  When the roses droop and die,
And their trembling petals faint,
  Odors float on every sigh,
        Without taint.

Pleasures live not till they 're gone.
  Song—its silent harmony—
Takes ethereal virtue on,
  Heard in thought and memory,
        Clothed upon.

Clothed upon ! Ah, who can know
  How the Spirit clothes upon
In this shadowy world below?
  Only in the heavenly dawn
        Shall we know !

FROM THE "COUNCIL GROUND."

SLEEPY-HOLLOW.

TO S. W. D.

I thank thee for the name, and for the spell
   Which thy weird fancy conjures, wherewithal
   To people this charmed spot ; for, as I call,
In answer, from the depths of yonder dell,
Sage chiefs, of forest fame, with warrior-yell
   Proclaim their sovereignty ; while softly fall,
   From lips of dusky maid,—that half enthrall,—
Wild notes of legendary song, to tell
   The tale of Love, Immortal, to her Brave.
Then, as again I wave the mystic wand,
   I hold true converse with the one who gave
The name. We pass the pledge, and seal the bond
   To share the rhythmic graces of the heart,
   Which lurk beneath these minstrel forms of art.

A SONG WITHOUT WORDS.

Sometimes a silence breathes upon the air,
Full laden with a music mutely deep,
That lulls the senses to oblivious sleep;
No silvery chords or murmuring lips may dare
To vie in sweetness with this songster rare,
Or share its harmonies, which, voiceless, steep
The sacred revery of the heart, and keep
The spirit kindred to the spell of prayer.
The purest notes, trilled by impassioned voice,
Are wasted then upon the listless ear;
The wakened memory is left no choice
But to be wooed in flight to some old year,
When mother-lips in holy prayer were heard,
Or maiden love once spoke its sovereign word.

CONSTANCY.

Her presence breathed of sun-lit slopes,
    Sweet-faced, toward the west,
As when a sadness blends with hopes,
    For love that's laid to rest;
Not yet had years their darkening scroll
    Of grievous trouble left,
Youth scarce had claimed its parting toll,
    Or beauty been bereft.

And many questioned, each of each,
    "Why one so young and fair,
Should shun the common ways that teach
    What common natures share?"
Though life revealed before her eyes
    Its fond utopian schemes,
Or love unveiled with softest sighs,
    Its fancy-woven dreams,—

Her life had other signs for her,
    Her love had other gain;
Her heart was her interpreter,
    Which earth could not profane.
Alas! I knew that solitude,
    To her was doubly sweet,
That other hearts could not intrude
    Since one had ceased to beat!

THEKLA.[1]

She listened for the last that his lips should utter,
  Who came with the message of death to her ears;
No trembling sigh for the dole that it brought her
  Unloosened the seal to her fountain of tears.

The pale on the cheek, that so often had spoken
  With blushes for joy that her bosom had borne,
Now lurks, like the signet of death, to betoken
  The doom of the night for the hope of the morn.

O where have they borne him, her warrior-slain lover,
  Whom the siren of battle had lured from her breast?
Though far away, yet will she roam the world over,
  To the grave where, in gloom, they have laid him to rest.

She calls for her steed, ere the swoon of her sorrow
  Has slackened its hold on her languishing heart,
And speeding her flight, ah! "To-morrow, to-morrow,"
  She cries, "I shall find thee, and weep where thou art."

Far in a dim cloister, beside its dumb altar,
    There vainly she utters his name for relief ;
The mute walls awaken with sad tones that falter,
    But the stones are unstained with tears for her grief.

And lowly she bends to the shrine, as she murmurs
    The plight of her heart to the heart that has fled ;
Yet never will dawn Love's fair, sunny Summers,
    O never will answer the lips of the dead !

She breathes the sweet vows once so ardently given,
    She listens, alas, for a voice that is still ;
No heart has the tomb for a heart that is riven,
    'Tis only the spirit her spirit can thrill !

Cold, like the mute marble, her form as they find her,
    No earth-wooing solace her anguish could still,
Love claimed her its own, and no bond here could bind her,
    Ah ! only its spirit her spirit can thrill !

"AH, NO MORE IS LOVE!"

Ah, no more is love, I said,
For the heart I loved is dead !

The deft hand I oft have grasped,
By another hand is clasped ;
The false lips that I have kissed,
Now by other lips are pressed ;
And the bond that made us one,
Is forever more undone !

Once her dexterous voice would sing
To my ears the loves of Spring ;
Once those furtive, piercing eyes
Stirred my heart with sweet surprise ;
Once her treacherous promise given,
Oped a fancied glimpse of heaven ;
Now, alas, I am forlorn,
For the plight that is forsworn !

Never lived that heart for me ?
Never ? Oh it cannot be !
Not for me the kisses meant,
Nor the passion thrills they sent ?
Or those 'trancing eyes that shone,
Were they not for me, alone ?

Were those tender notes of song
But the triumph of her wrong?
Were her luring words intoned
With a depth they never owned?

O, that life should teach me this,
That a sting lurks in a kiss!
That within the fairest flower,
Love has ashes for its dower!
That the faded leaf I press
Never had an emeraldness!
That the heart for which I grieve,
Pledged me, only to deceive!

Ah, no more is love; farewell
To the one who wove the spell!

IN THE RAVINES OF THE CATSKILLS.

Through moss-grown rifts, along the clifts,
  The wild surge leaps in silvery splendor;
And sheeny sprays melt in the rays
  Of Autumn sunlights, sadly tender,
While high above, the tremulous murmurs fly,
And lift their liquid music to the sky.

Far up the crag the waters flag,
  And pool in hollow caverns under,

Then break, and dash, in noisy crash,
   Adown the dizzy deeps like thunder,
Till, faintly falling in the depths below,
In dying laughter they forever flow.

The daisies prink the plashy brink,
   And from the rocks and lichens hoary,
The golden-rod, with mimic nod,
   Torch-like, blooms in its silent glory;
The trembling aster lifts its starry eye,
To take its purple-violet from the sky.

Dull odors float o'er fen and moat,
   On winds that sigh through piny tresses;
White vapors fall, and mantle all,
   To melt again in dream-like fleeces;
A radiance gilds the azure dome of light,
With rarer beauty through the chasmed height.

The eagle sweeps above the steeps,
   Unchallenged by the haunts of mortals;
The birdlings fling their carolling
   Through many hidden sylvan portals;
And airy love revives in downy breasts,
To wing its songs beneath the frowning crests.

Dusk twilight falls o'er towering walls,
   That Nature reared in scarrèd ledges,
Whose sullen deeps and donjon-keeps
   Are wrought with wreaths of ferny hedges,

Where covert solitude, serene, has slept,
'Mid battling storms that, ages long, have swept.

And over all the sear leaves fall,
   Mute emblems of a dying beauty,
Yet over all the sweet thoughts call
   The heart to realms of holier duty,
Till in the mountain glow of Autumn breath,
The spirit dreams beyond the sigh of death.

O Eden springs, whose freshness brings
   Elysian promises of heaven,
Whose lone defiles and shadowy aisles,
   To waiting souls, are visions given,—
As paths of upper air, whose ways, if trod,
Divinely lead from nature up to God !

GARFIELD.

Braver than Roman sentinel
   He died, enduring to the last ;
No captain ever nobler fell,
   Nor Death a deeper shadow cast.

Prayers, none could reach the mystery,
   Though millions daily lifted theirs,
The morrow baffled yesterday,
   As if in scorn of tears and prayers.

He felt the deadly touch, and still,
  With master-strength, he braved the strife;
For, oh, he battled with the will
  Of Christian fortitude, for life!

His courage won from all the world,
  A hero's due, of homage great;
At half-mast now, the flags, unfurled,
  Are draped for him who lies in state.

Large-brained, but larger yet of heart,
  His broadening sympathy divined
The lore of Truth, and had the art
  To teach its lessons to mankind.

He sought no prize or praise of men,
  No selfish dream, no blazoned fame,
His grand ideal of human ken
  Was more than circumstance or name.

He saw beyond earth's narrow shore,
  And spurned the shallow sands of Time;
For, in a higher faith, he bore
  The spirit-life of trust sublime.

Alas, to honors lifted high!
  Scarce one-half year of hope and fear—
In which to do, and then to die—
  Has laid him on his lonely bier.

A nation mourns beside the tomb
  Of him who kept its high decree;
O Death, thou hast thy sting and gloom!
  O Grave, thou hast thy victory!

HEART-POSSESSED.

He breathed a song once to the ear—
  The ear, wherever it might be
  To hear the new-born minstrelsy,
With heart to feel, ere it could hear
    The song he sang;

And sent it on its lonely way
  (The song)—a silent way—but heard
  No more through the round world one word
Of his rapt dream, from that glad day,—
    So light it was.

Then deeper in the shade he went,
  Where from the copses he entoned
  A melody that part bemoaned
The fate that met the first he sent;
    Yet none would hear.

Still later, in the sun and shade,
  There half-between, with faultless art,
  He poised a song without a heart,

To which faint praise the critics paid—
"A dainty thing."

And fear and hope were lightly blent,
Till suddenly a darkness fell
Across his way with ominous knell,
When all his passioned soul, unpent,
In grief went forth.

Then, heart-possessed, he wrote, in pain,
A song that from the depths outflew,
On wings that dazed the cunning few,
But the great world caught up the strain
And sang the song!

OPTIMISM.

I dream through years, for the joys to come;
Through twilight dusk, for the gold of morn;
My barque veers towards her destined home,
As over the harbor-bar she 's borne.

I deem the voyage a lightsome task,
And laugh at winds, and mock the tide;
In mists of the sun and moon I bask,
And watch the roll of the ocean wide.

I watch the roll of the ocean wide,
   Nor think that on its level expanse
Somewhere, sometime, my vessel may hide
   And wreck in its mountain waves, perchance.

For I gaze beyond the stormy swell,
   Far, far to the verge of space and time ;
I only know of the hopes that well,
   I can only see the end, sublime !

AT LENGTH.

Weak, we murmur for strength ;
   Helpless, we crave for power ;
Dreaming, alas, at length,
   Of their doubly-gifted dower ;
Waiting for chance to throw
   Fortune and favor and fame
All at our feet, and so
   Gain us a coveted name.

Strength ?—we gaze at the hills,
   Awed at splendor of sight ;
The might of tempest thrills ;
   A heap of wealth is might :
We strive, we dream, we fail ;
   Our wayward fancies play

Through castles of air that pale
   In visions that fade away.

But strength, ah, where is it found,
   Large and abundant to bless?
Will it not come at a bound?
   What is it? who can express?
Conjurers murmur their spell
   Of magic for idle fools;
Truth is found in a well;
   Knowledge is taught in the schools.

But strength from year to year,
   Through darkness of midnight, strength,
When those we hold most dear
   In love, are lost at length;
When scorn, and hate, and pain,
   And woe distil their dole,
And hopes that whispered gain,
   Are dead in the fainting soul!

Strength—as to skylark's wing—
   Comes from resistance long;
Comes from the songs we sing;
   Comes from suffering wrong.
The more we beat the tides,
   The more we breast the winds,
Strength through our pulses glides,
   Strength all our spirit binds.

We waver, we faint, we fall,
   We rise, and we fall again ;
Life is a service, a thrall,
   Life is a cry and a pain ;
Joy and its opposite, grief,
   Faith and its counter, despair,
Rest and its burdened relief,
   Tension of action and prayer,
Play through the passions of life.
   Weakness is mother of strength ;
Out of thraldom and strife
   Strength shall issue at length !

IN MEMORY.

F. A. T.—1883.

Scarce had life a fruitage borne,
   Fruit of Heaven in life of his,
When the blighting breath forlorn,
   Touched him with its withering kiss—

Smote him unto death, and he
   Lies beneath the sward, alas !
Distant, by the western sea,
   Lost to earth and all that was.

Who may know—ah ! who can tell
   All the spirits his has blest ?

IN MEMORY.

Who the mantle wear that fell
    From him, dying in the west?

Rests he there in silence now;
    Urned in earth, and formless grown,
Where the Summer breezes blow,
    Where the Summer flowers are blown.

All unconscious he of those
    Who their crowns and crosses bring;
He has found, at last, repose,
    Mindless of the songs they sing.

O'er the spot where he was lain
    Nestlings prattle in the boughs;
Though the heart be locked in pain,
    Nature there its peace bestows.

Silent flows the river there,
    Southward winding evermore,
And the melodies of air
    Wing above the changeless shore.

On his turf the sunlight falls
    With the passing of the day;
On his turf the shadow falls
    As the day-star fades away.

On his turf the still moon shines
    Silvery from its swelling crest;

Haply there the myrtle twines,
 More luxuriant for his rest.

Year on year will come and go,
 Doling out the laden hours;
Summer's harvest, Winter's snow,
 Land of frosts and land of flowers;

Yet, O brother lost to me!
 Aye, I hear the low refrain
Of the river to the sea:
 " He will not come back again."

SEPTEMBER.

A shadow rests upon the fields
 As earlier suns are setting;
The corn has reached the tasselled age,
 Its silken tresses netting;
And now the Autumn season waits,
 In mellowing forms of fruitage,
To shed its ripened sheaves and spheres,
 And lapse to Winter's dotage.

The woodbine takes the westering tints—
 The hectic flush—ere dying;
The golden-rod, torch-like, flames up,
 The waning sun defying;

The Mother-Earth has worn her robe
  Of green and floral beauty,
Until, by heat and rains caressed,
  She's filled her round of duty.

The squirrels dart from wall to wall,
  Or balance on their haunches,
To nibble on the last year's store,
  And watch the chestnut branches ·
The katydids scold in the wood,
  In rough, falsetto voices,
Where tuneful notes of summer song
  Are hushed by harsher noises.

The night-owl, in the thicket, wails
  In tones of melancholy,
As if bemoaning in its age
  Its years of youthful folly;
The parent-robin broods alone
  Within the shadowy gloaming—
Thinking, perchance, of empty nests,
  And children gone a-roaming.

The red light from the harvest moon
  Illumes the stilly places;
The fleecy islands cast their shapes
  Above the forest spaces;
The hills are hung in misty veils
  Beyond the glistening river;

And fallow thoughts blend with the heart
   Of memory, dreaming ever.

So Nature, in her fitful moods,
   Conjures her fleeting splendor
To draw from out the harp of life
   The sadder tones and tender ;
And I, who know these lingering days,
   The days that crown September,
Summon the deeper thoughts, to wake
   The loves that I remember.

UNEXPRESSED.

More elusive than a dream ;
   Finer than a fairy's song,
Than a rift of sunny gleam
   Through the woodland's leafy throng ;

Subtle as a piercing glance,
   Dashed with tint of joy or pain,
Are the vivid thoughts that 'trance
   The dull rapture of the brain.

Fancies, without words to tell
   Whence they come, or where depart,—
Like wild odors in the cell
   Of the rose, they haunt the heart.

UNEXPRESSED.

What time in the lavish Spring
　　The glad bosom thrills with bliss,
Soft they glide on viewless wing,
　　Light, and vanish like a kiss.

Whisper of a joy that 's passed ;
　　Touch the secret of a tear ;
Gild a hope that cannot last ;
　　Lisp a name thou wouldst not hear.

Birdlings are they of the mind,
　　Leaving but a wizard trail ;
For, alas, thou canst not find
　　Where they lurk behind the veil.

Laughters from the eddying rill,
　　Murmuring a plaintive glee ;
Monotones that inly fill
　　From the billows of the sea.

Passions, laden with a sigh ;
　　Matchless sunsets in the soul ;
Sorrows that down deeply lie,
　　Which no earthly knell can toll.

Heights whereon, in heavenly mood,
　　Hearts may mount in rhapsody ;
Loves that poets oft have wooed
　　In a moment's ecstasy.

Songs without the voice they are;
  Music from a stringless lyre;
Flecks of light that, faint and far,
  Lure the longings of desire.

Spirits of the earth and sky,
  Plumed to clip the peopled air;
Seek not where they form or fly,
  Thou canst never fathom where.

Write them in a poet's rhyme?
  Bind them to the lips of men?
Chain them with the tether, Time?
  Nay, they 'll slip thy narrow ken!

INDIAN SUMMER.

A dreamy haze of light; a fair deceiver;
  A ghost of summer's solstice, whose feigned smile
Half counterfeits the real; ah, false retriever;
  Yet art a sweet consoler in thy guile.

What gentle warmth, what odors from the valleys
  Drug the duped senses with their luring stealth!
The fancy drinks again from May's sweet chalice,
  And revels in its fairy land of wealth.

It is the Autumn's dotage—mid-November—
   When skies, seductive, seem to woo the earth ;
When e'en the flowers, if living, would remember
   The softer airs that swayed them at their birth.

The flowers, alas ! their perfumes have departed :
   Along the streamlet's marge and upland path
Vainly I search for them, till, lonely-hearted,
   I pluck, despondingly, the aftermath.

Within the barren depths of woodland yonder
   I seem to hear the bluebirds carolling,
And silently through reedy thickets wander,
   To find there but the mockeries of Spring.

The thrushes, where are they, whose notes resounded
   When all the air was vocal in the June ?
Their echoes then, from hill to vale rebounded,
   But now are banished out of time and tune.

The strolling piper blows a shrilly whistle ;
   The hunter calls his dogs from hedge and quail ;
The maiden plucks the last-blown downy thistle,
   And homeward, singing, tracks the beaten trail.

The banners of the forest fields have faded,
   And rustle in the lowly ways beneath ;
The sleepy solitudes that once they shaded,
   Now, desolate, cherish them like some dead wreath.

And still the waning sunlit glories linger
    To fire the dying embers with their gleam,
Until Death touches all with ominous finger,
    And frowns with frozen visage on the dream.

What are these days to lives that feel their sadness?—
    Pale phantoms call them not; they breathe the past,
Of Summer steeped in radiance and gladness—
    The Paradise of earth, that could not last.

They hallow in the thought, as dear reminders,
    The youth, the loves, the friendships that are gone,
And teach the heart, though these are left behind us,
    To hold its treasures for another morn!

"AH, LOWLY SPEAKS THE VOICE OF DEATH."

Ah, lowly speaks the voice of Death,
    When on the heart it breaks,
Yet, how with woe it thrills the breath,
    And cries of anguish wakes.

It echoes love, but love that tells
    How vain is this of ours,

Whose throbbings mingle with sad knells,
    And perish with the flowers.

We stretch out blindly with our hands,
    We strain our eyes to meet
The eyes that dawn on viewless lands;
    The life we cannot greet.

O God, that we could give our own,
    In toils and hardships drear,
To win the spirit back that's flown,
    And hold its image near!

Yet Death, thou hast a meaning deep,
    Whose mystery, unsealed,
Would dry the eyes that vainly weep,
    And cure the hearts unhealed.

The secret of thy holier truth,—
    The faith sublimely great—
'Tis ours to learn through love and ruth,
    And patience that must wait.

HEART OF GOLD.

What matter, though the world be alien cold,
Though to the finer senses it but deign
A cheerless answer, making light of gain
That stirs our swift, divining thoughts, to hold
Us thrall in some sublimer wish untold?
What matter, so that music yield its strain
To thrill, fair love its rapture and its pain,
And the vast future pledge its heart of gold?
Though the deft schemes of men may sink to loss,
Though withering care may sere the edge of sense,
Though jeweled fortune fade to feathery dross,
If but these soul-lit joys remain intense,
Freighted with longing, winged with Argos sails,
Deem not that life is barren, Heaven avails!

WOMAN-WISE.

Man is not wise above the rarer grace
Of woman-wise. To wield his weapons wrought
Of steely metal drawn from polished thought ;
With well-trained speech to run some wordy race,
Or sturdily with iron will to trace
Some drudging task that early he was taught,—
These are his powers, from the world's armory brought.
But hers are spirit-shielded, as in lace ;
Elastic, free, on intuition's wing
Of radiant thought she says her sweeter say ;
Her heart-life melodies, inbreathing, sing
To dreams the " heat and burden of the day,"
While love, ethereal, endows her sphere,
And makes her wiser than the wisest seer.

LOVE'S FAITH.

Beneath the shadow of the hill,
   On eastern slopes, she sings and sighs;
And waiting by the lonely rill,
   Her pulse with its wild ripple vies.

The birds that westward take their flight,
   And every wind that sweeps the sea,
Bear on their courses toward the night
   Some message from her heart to thee.

To thee! for in the golden mists
   Of the far western clime, is one
Who waits, but waits in vain, and wists,
   And dreams and muses of his own.

By every barque that sets its sail,
   On all the tides that eastward flow,
He answers, through the calm or gale,
   A love that only two can know.

From west to east, from east to west,
   The birds they fly, the tides reply;
Two hearts, alas! may never rest,
   For love that waits but cannot die.

And, fainter, murmur o'er the sea
  Two voices that are never still:
"O maid, I may not come to thee,
  Nor woo thee by thy lonely rill."

And she: "Thy lips I may not kiss,
  In eyes of thine may never gaze,
But Heaven will crown a love like this,
  That vainly waits through earthly days."

BROKEN-HEARTED.

She gathered buds in the maiden June,
  For her coronal of bridal flowers;
Her bosom throbbed as it kept in tune
  With songs of birds to the matin hours.

The wreath she wove was moistened with dew,
  With tears of joy from her love-lit eyes.
Her lips moved to a song that was new,
  A song for the morning's sun to rise.

She plucked the green from the ivied wall,
  She twined its sheaves in her waving hair,
To wait the voice of her lover's call;
  The flush on her cheek was crimson fair.

O doomful hours that die in the shade,
   Ere the virgin web of life is spun ;
O crimson cheeks that sicken and fade,
   For grief that wakes ere another sun.

He never came ; to her fevered sense
   No dews revived the flowers at night ;
The moon shone not, for her wild suspense
   Had dimmed her eyes to its silvery light.

She took no heed of the night-bell's toll,
   The perfume from her blossoms was gone ;
The morrow's sun had set in her soul
   Ere she saw its radiant glory dawn.

The seasons that passed were lost to her ;
   For her no Autumn its harvest shed ;
In her Winter-breast the chill frosts were ;
   Her heart of love was silent and dead.

She plucked the green from the ivied wall,
   But oh, the green of another day !
She saw the seared leaves flutter and fall,
   As love from her life had fallen away.

The long year passed ; in a maiden June
   They twined young blossoms, to crown her hair ;
E'en the birds seemed sad and out of tune—
   They missed her song in the lonely air.

Save murmuring brook or breeze, no sound
    Disturbs the vale where they laid her low;
Wild flowers steal softly from her mound—
    Earth's angels—to watch, who loved her so.

LONGFELLOW.[5]

[March 24, 1881.]

His day is spent, and he is dead;
The Nestor-poet's silvered head
Is lying low, as sad and slow,
They bear him to his hollow bed.

His lips a voiceless silence keep;
He sleeps, alas, a mortal sleep;
His rayless eye cannot reply
To other eyes that vainly weep.

No more, through sinuous tones, his song,
In fresh-drawn notes shall move along;
No magic theme through him shall dream
In rhythmic music to the throng.

We call it Death;—it cannot be!
From land to land, from sea to sea,
A wingèd fame has borne his name;
No Death can still his minstrelsy.

O, poet of the golden lyre,
O, glory of our western choir,
Thy living page, from age to age,
Shall light with an immortal fire!

THE CLOUDED MIND.

I know not when the glory fled—
   The spirit-light that filled his mind,
But now its rays are dark and dead,
   His words are strange, his thought is blind.

I speak his name, no voice replies;
   I gaze into his eyes, and lo,
They but return their blank surprise
   For loving looks of long ago!

He murmurs in some alien tone
   The wild falsetto of his brain,
As reason, fettered on its throne,
   Laments its hapless bonds in vain.

I sing familiar songs, I read
   The chosen books he once had known;
Alas! they but enhance the need;
   I sing and read as if alone.

THE CLOUDED MIND.

Sweet friendships and companions dear
  Are banished from his soul distraught;
His world is closed to joy and fear,
  And love is exiled from his heart.

With aimless wanderings,—as in dreams—
  He gropes through fields and forest ways,
He strolls along the lowland streams,
  And counts the hours of vacant days;

Yet sometimes, when the Autumn light
  Sinks, deepening, in the western skies,
I hear, as from the lowering night,
  A vagrant note of sadness rise;

A sudden gleam, a moment's boon,
  Has touched his thought, as now he sings
Some snatch, some fragment of a tune
  That memory out of chaos brings.

Then, on his lonely life again,
  The brooding shadows denser fall,
To quench the spark that lit his brain,
  To shroud it in their midnight pall.

Still waiting, waiting, longingly,
  As years of endless days go past,
I watch for reason's mild decree,—
  For light and love to reign at last.

THE MYSTERY.

Cold winds of Winter swept the place
   Where one, in grief, had borne her own ;
   The frosts had sheathed each marble stone,
And chilled the tears upon her face.

She laid the little form to rest
   Whose soul had gone to Him who gave ;
   She bent above the open grave,
And felt the void within her breast.

Ere yet the moon had waned, and lo !
   Another of her life was slain
   Of Death, that palled her heart again,
And smote it with a tearless woe.

Two lay together, side by side,
   And o'er their winter mounds were wreathed
   The buds that parting love bequeathed,
Dying, alas ! as they had died.

Sometime from those two mounds shall spring,
   From living stems, the buds again,
   Updrawn by Summer's suns and rain,
Blossoms of Nature's nurturing.

"Sometime," the childless mother said,
"My waiting heart may go to mine,
Where, cherished by a thought divine,
The loves shall blossom that are dead."

1863–1883.

GREETING.

I give thee greeting—thou, my wedded heart;
Through the fair seasons of so many a year
Thou hast bestowed thy benediction dear,
On a more shadowed life than thine; thou art
A sunny clime, a light that dost impart
Thy radiance with more than blithesome cheer;
A golden lining, when dark clouds appear,—
To shed thy rays, unconscious of the art.
Though all else fail, thy constancy will last;
The bond that holds us thrall I may not plead,
'Tis tried and true, and needs no verse or rhyme;
I gaze into thy face, I hold thee fast,
I print love's kiss on thy sweet lips, and lead
Thee forth through all the shoals and deeps of time!

AT SUNSET.

SONGS WITHOUT WORDS.

Soft, like a stolen calm, their echoes rest,
Above the worn and grievous burdened soul :
The harsh world loses now its dull control ;
O, rapt Imagination, thou art blest !
Out of the molten glory of the west,
From the low sunset-bells that faintly toll,
Commingling, as in one dear, ransomed whole,
Comes now the music that I love the best—
Music without the noisy organ-peal,
Without the chorus or the dulcet string,
Unwritten, silent to the sensuous ear,
Strains all unheard, but which the heart can feel,
Vague voices of the memory, murmuring
The tears and laughters in some halcyon year.

FIDELITY—A SONG.

The heart that must ever possess her
   Is exiled to ocean deeps,
And the love that never can bless her
   A fathomless silence keeps.
Yet the wild sea-surge, in its sighing,
   Has whispered no pang to her breast,
While hope in her bosom, undying,
   Beats high in its billowy rest.

No mirth ever melts her to laughter,
   No melody thrills her with bliss;
But a thought of her lover comes after,
   And mingles her spirit with his.
Her longing, unburdened by sorrow,
   No fear of her fancy can dim;
Her tears are the dreams of to-morrow
   That crystal with visions of him.

She listens to the songsters of Summer,
   To the fitful fountains at play,
And lends to their musical murmur
   A song to her love far away.
She hears, in the cadence of ocean,
   His passion low-voiced in the wave,

And breathes him a double devotion,
   A seal for the troth that she gave.

Alas for the rose of the morning !
   The night-frost withers its bloom ;
Or the lustre of hope in its dawning,
   (A phantom that fades in the gloom) ;
And alack for the years that are wasted
   In music that dies on the air—
For a bliss that never is tasted,
   For a joy that wanes to despair !

She sits by the sea in the gloaming ;
   She sighs for her lover of yore ;
Her heart o'er the ocean is roaming,
   As she waits on its desolate shore ;
Yet the love that never can bless her
   A fathomless silence keeps :
The heart that must ever possess her
   Is exiled to ocean deeps.

"MUTE THY LIPS."

Clay thou art, a lifeless thing,
    Hands and feet and form of earth;
Clay thou art, the fatal sting
    Robbed thee of thy precious worth.

To the grave they bore thy dust,
    O'er thy bier they read the rite;
Ah! so soon thy likeness must
    Crumble from my eager sight!

"Where," I asked, "has fled the ray
    From thy soft, entreating eye?
What cold fate has borne away
    The deep passion-laden sigh?

"Where are Love and Sorrow gone,—
    Banished from thine empty breast?
In what viewless realm, forlorn,
    Art thou waiting to be blest?

"Where the music of thy song?
    Where the Heaven of thy prayer?
Do they to the earth belong,
    Only its frail dreams to share?"

"Comes no answer from the tomb?
   Hast no message, thou, to tell
Of elysian shades, in bloom,
   Where the mystic spirits dwell?

" Comes no word to mortal men?"
   Mute thy lips!—O, could they speak,
What diviner thoughts would then
   Crown a faith that is so weak!

Yet, alas! I cannot say;
   Only this, my Love, my Own,—
Since thy soul has led the way,
   Mine must follow thine, alone!

"SKY-TOP."

The birds had left their mountain nests;
   The air was still; no throb of song
   Beat its pulsation clear, along
The old, deserted, crannied rests.

The birds had left; I wondered why,—
   Why in those lofty crowns of Time,
   Where Nature's grandeur sleeps sublime,
The birds disdained to live and die.

I wondered why the dainty " blue,"
    The thrush, the oriole, the jay,
    Had flown from their wild cliffs away,
To lowly haunts and valleys new.

Ah, sweet, we upward, upward fly!
    We seek the skyey tops; we strain
    Our eyes afar to span the plain,
And yet—and yet, I wonder why

We turn us to the vales below—
    Of earth—and cherish their dull wealth?
    Why glean their fruits, as if by stealth
To hoard the treasures they bestow?

Poor human thought, it cannot rise;
    It sinks, it falters as it climbs;
    Its music lacks the heavenly rhymes,
Its sense is dazzled with the skies.

The valleys call and it obeys;
    Forgetting its diviner birth
    It craves the glory of the earth,
And follows in the beaten ways:

Then why not birds? They, too, may long,
    While dreaming on the mountain pine,
    Unmindful of their home divine,
To win earth's fortunes for a song.

H. W. L.

MARCH 24, 1882.

A flower bloomed forth in a western land,
   With petals of lily, and gold, and rose;
It scattered its seeds on every hand,
    And laded the air with its perfumed blows;
      It sent its shoots o'er heather and fen,
      And gladdened the common ways of men.

Its rhythmic colors, and magic charm,
   In manifold mixture of beauty blent:
It bore in its heart a healing balm;
    Some said it was an exotic sent,
      And others, who missed its secret dower,
      Declared it only a common flower.

The wind, the heat, the night, and the rain,
   All tempered it with their mellowing clime;
The seasons came and went again,
    As it bloomed afresh in the blight of time;
      Its heralds sped far o'er sea and shore,
      And around the world its banners bore.

Wherever the eye of man could see,
   Or ever the soul of man could feel,

There blossomed its beauteous harmony,
  And there its chaliced virtue to heal;
    Its heart was in the land of its birth,
    But its gentle spirit pervaded the earth.

Then there came a season, a day, an hour,
  When its ripened lustre dimmed and died;
Men mourn the loss of the peerless flower,
  That healed, and sweetened, and beautified;
    Sometime the world, outwearing its grief,
    The flower will find in a fadeless sheaf.

THE FLOWER AND THE TREE.

Sad poetess she who sings in the shade
  Of grief that is born to the ripening years;
Who'd bloom, like the flower, to droop and to fade
  Ere bitterness blind her soul with its tears;

Who would burden the air with odorous sweets
  From the cell of the fairy's secret nook,
Or bud and blossom in Eden retreats,
  To revel in dreams with the birds and the brook;

To hold the chalice of joy to the skies
  And catch the sun and the dew in its brim,
To toy with the bees and the gold butterflies,
  Or nod to the loves that answer her whim;

To live in beauty, to languish and die,
    Exhaling her soul on the summer breath,
No question to ask of the mystery, why
    She bore the burden of life and of death.

Methinks I would grow, with the passage of time,
    Like the nobler tree, till my deepening bands
Should steal the spoil of the loam and the lime,
    And feed on the heart of the teeming lands.

Till my stripling years were passed, and the wind
    Might temper my foils in its eager chase,
And the storms might blind, and the tempest bind,
    And grapple me in its mighty embrace.

Then the sun might fire my heart with its own,
    And Winter impale with its icy bars ;
Then the night might fall and leave me alone,
    I'd welcome the fire, the frost, and the stars.

So they fill and thrill my life with their balm,
    And blend their subtle emotions to train
My sinewy form in a passionate calm,
    I'd drink of their spirit and vanquish the pain.

Ah, then, when I'd won, through travail and toil,
    The kingdom of earth, with its rich empire,
I'd plead exemption and peace from its moil,
    And longingly breathe my prayer of desire.

SEEDS, THE ENGINEER.

Seeds was the man on the Penn. Railroad ;
    Seeds was the engineer ;
Six hundred souls behind him rode,
    When the flames shot out to the rear ;
The flames flashed out from the engine's breath,
    And fired the laden air ;
To stay at his post was worse than death,
    To fly was the hope of despair.

With a dash he cleared the deadly heat
    And stood on the foremost car,
While his engine flew o'er the iron street
    Like a devil let loose for war.
Six hundred panic-stricken hearts
    In breathless horror wait,
As the train, with thund'rous rumblings, darts
    And bounds along to its fate.

Seeds was the one, the only man
    To check the demon race ;
He stood like a statue in the van
    With the glare of the flame in his face,
Not a muscle moved ; a look of disdain,
    A shudder—but not for fear,—

Then a plunge in the hell of fire again
   To his post as engineer.

The hush of the shadow of death was there ;
   Hope hung by a single thread ;
A minute seemed longer than a year—
   That minute of terrible dread ;
A grating sound, a slackened speed,
   A swaying to and fro,
And a hero had saved, by a hero's deed,
   Who knows, of nameless woe !

A seared form, naked, and speechless, and faint,
   Crept out of the fiery mass ;
'Twas Seeds. Ah, noble as ever a saint,
   He who braved that terrible pass !
Let his memory haunt the hearts of men
   In scorn of their selfish greed,
And the world shall echo its great Amen !
   For the crowning of his deed.

VICTORY.

Say not that absence dissipates
   The bond that makes two spirits one;
   That love is true of earth, alone;
That death must sever human fates;
   I know a friend whose simple ways—
   And blest, outlive her mortal days.

Death touched her, but through years of grace
   The spirit, clinging by a thread
   To her frail image, hourly shed
Its beauty in her soul and face;
   A ray from some divine light, given
   To link and lead her life to heaven.

Sweet words were hers, no other speech
   So gentle, bearing, like the flowers
   That fade within the fleeting hours,
A fragrance far beyond their reach;
   Words, too, that lips may not express,
   Save from a fount of loveliness.

No poor pretence, no mocking deeds
   Of charity, for others' praise,

Were feigned by her; no vain displays
To win fair words; she knew the needs
  That pressed the lowly to despair,
  And brought her gifts with them to share.

If beauty came from God, she knew
  That beauty only came with good;
  Her rarer nature understood
The graces hid from human view;
  The gospel scheme of life, with her,
  Must needs be wrought in character.

Her crowning victories were defeat;
  Her highest joys were born in pain;
  Her reverent sorrowings were gain;
Fit fruitage for a soul so meet,
  Wearing its bitter weeds, content
  That they were given—divinely sent.

Serene and beautiful, at peace,
  Though burdened, caring but for this,
  That all her days might be like His,
Till heaven should bring its sweet release;
  Unmurmuring for the thorns that press,
  Since earth would end in blessedness.

I plucked fresh flowers, on that calm morn,
  To wreathe her grave, yet felt it true

That thought would blossom, ever new,
With fragrant memories of her, gone:
   That in near, friendly hearts would spring
   Love's flowers, more fair than hands could
      bring.

NOVEMBER.

There is no blossom in the field;
   The fierce winds lash the naked wood;
Barren and cold, the gray hills yield
   Their hearts to winter solitude;
Night folds its dusk across the sheen of day,
And bleak November sows the seed of May.

Wild storms and ghostly echoes wake
   The sullen silence. Nature's smile
Plays on a frozen face, to break,
   Despairingly, the gloom, awhile,
Then dips behind its snowy veil of cloud—
That sifts adown to earth an ermine shroud.

November sows the seed of May;
   But ere the germ shall feel the spell,
The touch that pulses into play,
   Death lays it in a narrow cell;
Death holds it fast in Winter's icy breath,
In Winter's tomb, till life is born of death.

O Hope, exiled to hopelessness,
   Pierced by the chill, the ghost of May,
Smitten where once thou felt a kiss,
   Night-blinded where was glorious day,
Thou, too, must die of frost, and press the tomb
Awhile, ere yet thy life may come to bloom.

THE OLD AND THE NEW.

I hear the birds singing blithely, the birds of a vanished June,
   And green are the boughs, and sweet are the vows
That mix in the airy tune,
And the radiant glory of Summer,
   In its flush, untarnished fire,
Is mingled with passions that murmur
   With an affluence of desire.

Still lingers the violet's beauty ; the odor of its perfume
   Floats upward, away, on the wings of May,
To blend in the golden loom ;
And the heart of the lover is wooing,
   And the heart of the maiden yields,
Till the lips, full-ripened with suing,
   Are kissing in blooming fields.

I hear the voices of children in the noon of the
    silent year,
  Their faces I see, and their laughter and glee
I hear, yet I do not hear.
Ah! children, thy tones, like a spirit,
  Fade away, as a dream that has fled.
Their echo, how faintly I hear it,
  Through the aisles of the year that is dead!

And Autumn has gone, with its harvest; its crim-
    son, hectic leaves
  Lie withered in death, in the frosty breath,—
For the reapers have gathered their sheaves;
And the gales of wild December
  Bear their waves against the sky,
But the loves that I remember
  Shall never—ah! never die!

How bleak are the hills and forests, like a shadow
    on the heart!
  The birds and their lay have died away,
With the year so loath to depart;
Yet there comes from whither—oh! whither,
  A faith that heralds a day
When never again shall wither
  The loves and the longings of May;

When lilies will bloom forever, and beauty will
    never pale;
  When the songs of June will keep in tune

With hopes that never will fail;
When the voices of children, forever,
  Will sound through the blessèd spheres,
And death no more will sever
  The loves of earthly years!

"GIVE US, THIS DAY."

"Give us, this day, our daily bread," unthinking, said
The child at night; the meaning of the upward flight
  Of that low prayer, it could not tell;
  It knew the words by heart, so well,
Yet, bending at its nightly shrine, could not divine
The heavenly theme, which seemed a far-off wonder-dream.

The years they swiftly came and fled; unheeding said
The youth, again, the prayer that seemed not all in vain,
  "Give us, this day, our daily bread;"
  And brightly shone about his head
The gloried happiness of earth,—its joy and mirth;
The bread it came, though prayer to him was but a name.

The child, the youth, to manhood grew, and
    rougher blew
The storms of life, and deepening sorrow, sterner
    strife,
  Bore down upon his toiling brain;
  " Give us our daily bread," again
He said; the answer came in death, that hushed
    the breath
Of one his love had worshipped more than all
    above.

And swiftly, yet, the answer came, as in a flame,
To try his soul, and from his eager grasp it stole
  The jewelled fortune he had wrought;
  And, as, again, he blindly sought,
By utterance of the daily prayer, the daily share
Of bread to win, there came a vision of his sin.

And now, whene'er the prayer he said, there rose
    the dead
One in his heart. " O God, thy hand hath sent the
    dart;
  But she whose steps I oft have led,
  I hear her voice,—she is not dead;
In ceaseless murmurs of the sea, she whispers me;
In every prayer her spirit guides my spirit there."

"Give us, this day, our daily bread," the worn man
    said;
His weary soul now toiled no more for earthly toil;

Now he had found the holy bread
Above the wreck of earthly dead ;
Beyond the valley of despair, beyond the prayer,
A Christly light illumed the way,—it was not night.

Age whitened on his crested brow ; a heavenly vow
Long years had led his soul in prayer for heavenly bread.
  The Cross, in him, was lifted high,
  A sign of faith that could not die ;
Till in his life it wrought a calm, a nameless charm,
And still he said, "Give us, this day, our daily bread."

THE UNSENT MISSIVE.

  In a dingy attic room,
    'Midst its lumbered solitude—
  Brooding in its musty gloom,
    Sat a man in dreamy mood
      There, alone ;—
  Holding in his hand a letter
    Written years agone.

THE UNSENT MISSIVE.

Neither old nor young was he,
   Scarcely wrinkled, touched with gray,
Bachelor of third degree,
   Past the age—ah, well-a-day!
     And he read,—
From the oaken chest a letter;
   Something from the dead.

Pale was he, for there his vow,
   " Love thee," written by his hand;
Dated years ago, till now
   Left unbroken, seal and band,
     Made to her,—
He a lover, tender-hearted,
   Wrote it once, to her.

Twenty years, alas! had gone:
   Resting on his hand awhile,
Mused he of the halcyon morn,
   Felt the radiance of her smile;
     Where was she?
Her sweet face, almost forgotten,
   Would he ever see?

Twenty years the missive lay
   Lost, while he had thought it sent
On its mission; day by day,
   Bitter in his discontent,
     Waited he

For the coming of her answer :
　　Cursed the maiden he !

Then he lived in scorn of her,—
　　Till, corroding in his breast,
Hate had left him shorn of her
　　For a passion never blest ;
　　　　Now, a change,
In a flood of memory, thrilled him
　　　　With emotion strange.

Love came back, and hatred fled ;
　　Form and face and accent now,
Came to him from out the dead,—
　　With the sealed and banded vow.
　　　　Love—the truth—
Lost and found, an unread secret,
　　　　From the heart of youth.

But the maiden, she had gone :
　　Only there her image dwelt,
A mute phantom inly born,
　　Ever seen and ever felt,
　　　　Blessed ideal—
In the current of his being—
　　　　Came to be the real.

Wed was he forevermore ;
　　Life and love and spirit wed ;

Could not seek her, dare not know her,
  Living, she to him were dead.
    Memory wrought
Her fair vision, as an angel's,
  In his world of thought.

WASHINGTON IRVING.[1]

1783–1883.

Distant we stand, as if, from some far main,
We viewed a wide expanse of wave and strand,
Till, midway in the Eastern glimpse of land,
Our vision greets a mountain on the plain.

Time, distance, cannot veil our wistful eyes,
The lofty peak stands ever as before,
And we, while gazing from the level shore,
See, now, its form in stainless lustre rise.

Clear sky and golden beauty bathe the height,
Serene it lifts its airy crest to fame,
Above the need or care of praise or blame,—
A fadeless summit clothed in robes of light.

So stands our Irving of a hundred years,
Loved master in the field of lettered lore,

Whose brow first bore the crown, and nobly wore
Its circling nimbus far above his peers.

He missed the unsheathed sword, the battle plain,
That won for liberty her fair increase,
But kept his birthday in the year of peace,—
The nation's jubilee from strife and pain.

He taught our embryo empire in its youth,
That art was loyal to its natal cause ;
And wrote of gentler manners, kindlier laws,
Of beauty bred in common ways of truth.

From the wild haunts of brooding solitude,
From old traditions steeped in romance dear,
He brought his marvels to the duller ear,
And in the heart a finer fancy wooed.

He had the poet's music and his dream,
His wanton imagery, without his song,
Yet deftly wrought, in rhythms pure and strong,—
Idyllic like—the legend of his theme.

To him was given the charmed magician's hand,
To weave, with all, a mystic tale of love,
Or some sweet spell, the spirit-life to move,
And win it captive by his potent wand.

An affluent soul was his, that made man kin,
A genial humor graced with beauteous speech,

Evoking tears and laughter, blessed to teach
A purer accent to the voice within.

What fair creation has his genius wrought!
What witcheries—in peopling yon lone vale—
He wove into the texture of a tale,
And fashioned in the fancy of his thought!

The tides that bore him once to Eastern lands,
Come back to-day, resounding, as they came
Long years ago, with echoes of his name,
And sweep their messages across our sands.

Till we, within the shadow of his home,
Bless the full radiance of his renown,
That breaks, benign, beyond the sea and town,
Unvexed by other lights that go and come.

And, through the centuries, we see afar,
His glory—nothing dimmed from age to age—
In panegyrics, light the living page,
To pledge for him the orbit of a star.

NIGHT WATCHES.

Only the shrouding gloom can unfold
The skyey chart with its worlds of gold;
  Only the darkness can make the night
  A fathomless miracle of light!

Only the shadow of night in the heart
Reveals to the soul the heavenly chart;
  Only the darkness that falls at our feet
  Can make the meaning of God complete!

CHRISTMAS.

I've heard the lark in Summer, wingèd high,
  Sing in the heavenly ether till, ere long,
It seemed to melt—a spirit in the sky—
  Still pouring forth its liquid notes of song.

I've heard in Autumn months the throstle sing
  A very harvest song, so tender sweet!
As if, in blissful joyance, it would bring
  A heartful sacrifice of praises meet.

But in the Winter, when the year is old,
    And birds have flown, and the broad, barren earth
Is bound in frigid bands, and bitter cold,—
    When all is dead, the heart warms into mirth ;

And anthemed voices choir, and CHRIST is sung ;
    The bells ring wildly through the crispy air ;
The breezes waft it, 'tis on every tongue,—
    'Tis Christmas ! Merry Christmas everywhere !

"THE DEAD YEAR."

Along the shores of Time the lights are burning
That mark the distant years, long time we sped,
The years that now are dead.
No alchemy of life shall herald their returning,
Those fragments wrecked by the "relentless hand"
Far on the wasted strand.

How dimly burn the lights ! till now, there glistens
One more, one more to mock the hollow eye
Of Time's departed sage.
In vain, in vain the ear of memory listens,
For only silence echoes back again
The heart's own voiceless strain.

THE DEAD YEAR.

And is the past a dream, some peopled vision?
Is it the phantom of a pageant gone?
Has it no other morn?
No life beyond this fleet delusive mission?
Is nothing left but some historic scroll,
The ashes of the soul?

The song, the sigh, the inward, nameless sorrow;
The death-throb of some heart, some blessed friend;
The wrong, the right amend,
That held the conscience clear, in the to-morrow;
The wild joy fired by some ambitious scheme,—
Are these an idle dream?

The high trust born, the strong hope knit to heaven,
The faith transcendent, conquering the grave;
The sacrifice to save;
The crescent love from heart to heart once given,—
Is none of all this subtle influence, spent,
To some fair future lent?

Sure, every day is a divine presaging;
Nor art, nor life is lost to human good;
Even our daily food
Decrees some ransom than the sheer assuaging
Of the hungered flesh, as sap to flower
Yields an ethereal dower.

O count not waste the year that has departed,
For its fair beauty here, shall reappear

In some sublimer sphere,
Its frailest good shall leave men fuller-hearted,
And the pure essence of its earthly spell
Live after its own knell.

"ABIDE WITH ME."

"Abide with me, fast falls the eventide,"
A simple maiden sang, with artless feeling;
"The darkness deepens, Lord, with me abide,"
While in her voice the tender accents stealing,
   Fell, softly as the dying day,
   From those sweet lips, and died away.

"Abide with me," she could not know the plea,—
The utter consecration,—in her dreaming;
Joy, like a bird, made life a melody,
And Spring, its sun, along her pathway beaming,
   Stirred her young heart with gentle fires,
   And quickened it with sweet desires.

"The darkness deepens," slowly fell the sound,
As if with plaintive grief the notes were laden,
Yet not a sorrow had her bosom owned,
Nor ever sadness touched the lovely maiden;
   How could she sing "Abide with me,"
   Or know its hidden mystery?

"The darkness deepens," and the years go by ;
The maiden 'neath the shadows oft has wandered ;
Joy, like a bird, has left its nest to fly,
And bonds of love and happiness are sundered ;
   Lo, all the friendliness of earth
   Has taken wings, with joy and mirth.

Despair, the tearless offspring of all woe,—
The lonely progeny of a world of sorrow,—
Has turned upon her, like a sudden foe,
To snatch Hope's only legacy—To-morrow ;
   And, shuddering, in her dumb distress,
   She drinks the cup of bitterness.

O Life ! she knows the anguish of its cross,—
Love turned to hate, and blessings to reverses,—
She, too, has felt the fever of remorse,
With its deep dregs of agony and curses ;
   "When helpers fail and comforts flee,"
   She dare not plead, " Abide with me."

Her voice, it will not sing, the notes are dead ;
But in their stead, like some pale phantom, haunting,
Weird echoes, through her memory, mocking dread,
Breathe the dead song her aching heart is wanting ;
   "Abide with me" she cannot sing,
   But mutely brings the offering.

"Fast falls the eventide" ; yet, to her eyes,
The golden light of morn is faintly dawning ;

"Earth's joys grow dim," but from eternal skies
Is borne the answer to her spirit's longing;
   And now, as "falls the eventide,"
   She whispers, "Lord, with me abide."

She knows it now, the faith that comes at last;
Child of the pang and travail of her spirit,
Born of the withering passions of the past,
Its Heavenly Voice, she lingers long to hear it;
   Lo, through the Valley of Despair,
   Her song has sung itself to prayer!

NAY, TOUCH THEM NOT.

Far have I wandered, and the silent way
O'erpassed is strewn with life-thoughts, new and old;
Some half-remembered, like mute graves with mold
And mosses mingled with the lichens gray;
Some vivid, young with life of yesterday;
And some deep, soulful-born, that fain would hold
The vaster meanings of the spirit-world,
Celestial-winged, nor kin with time or clay.
These all are mine, and with them life and love;
And would I change them, new and old, or mar
Or blur their vision in the memory?
Nay, touch them not, nor one dull dream remove.
Each, like the heavenly orb of each still star,
Forevermore gleams in its realm for me.

LOVE-BOUND.

I felt the scorn within her breast,
    And scorn, it burned within my own ;
Her look ! I read it, and I guessed
    The bitter sentence in her tone.
Not harsh—that silvery voice was pure
    And cold, I thought, as winter frost.
Her eyes, in my gaze, seemed to lure
    Like false lights, to the seamen lost.

Yet never beauty shone as hers,
    In that proud form and pallid face ;
Earth has its peerless characters,
    But none could match her perfect grace.
Unmoved, she like a statue stood ;
    She spoke in low and measured breath :
" My dear sir, you are very good,
    But loveless hearts are worse than death.

" I give you back this jewelled band,
    Its pledge renounce ; they're yours—what more ?
You've kept your heart ; I claim my hand :
    Henceforth forget the love of yore."
Henceforth forget ! Ah, vain her speech !
    How mad my thought ! I turned at bay,
And though she stood within my reach,
    She seemed the breadth of seas away.

She trembled, all her nature thrilled,
    Spell-bound, like one rapt in a trance ;
Her lips were colorless and stilled,
    And pain was written in her glance.
Then, with untrammelled voice again,
    The color mounting to her cheek,
She spoke : "You need not seek in vain ;
    Go, other hearts like mine are weak.

"If love is but a lightsome game,
    A fancy for an idle mood,
Go, warm you by its fickle flame,
    Then break the heart that you have wooed.
But know that love is heaven-born,
    A passion guarded by a law ;
A rose defended by a thorn,
    A sacred thing to answer for.

"If you would claim it, you must wear
    It nobly ; not as gift of earth ;
Its spirit you can never snare,
    And beauty is but half its worth."
I heard the stinging words she spoke,
    A silence for a moment's pause
Sealed up my answer ; then I woke ;
    I urged the secret of her cause ;

"What venomed lips have lied to thee ?
    What false words, whispered to thine ear,

Have turned thy virgin love from me,
  To poison with a heartless jeer?
I know not; let them cursèd be.
  Some gossip from the baser born,
Has wrought, through foulest perfidy,
  To blacken all the hopes of morn!

" Henceforth, since thy sweet faith has fled,
  What matter that our love is lost?
'Tis better that we never wed,
  Than pay its price at such a cost.
'Tis better that we never wed,
  If every wind can bear a tale
To shake the calm, and fill with dread
  Of angry storm, our love-lit sail!"

I saw the melting of her snow,
  I felt the throbbing of her heart.
Love flamed her bosom with its glow,
  And bound us that we could not part!

NEWBURGH, OCTOBER 18, 1883.

I hear the bells ring out their mirth,
   In gladdening melodies, and clear,
Breaking the stillness of the earth,
   And sending welcome to the year.

The thundering cannon belch their fire
   From upland reaches near and far,
And music breaks from trump and lyre,
   To soften the tumultuous jar.

A hundred years ago, and peace
   Was shouted through a mourning land ;
Men wept with joy that war should cease,
   Tear-blinded, clasping hand in hand.

Long had the new land, prone, and wrung
   With dreary and despairing woe,
Heard but the sadder requiems sung,—
   Still struggling with a deadly foe.

Then hope died with each dying year
   Of waste, and shed no promised light ;
Then faith was overcast by fear,
   And courage wrought through gloom and night !

The musket and the delving spade
   A desolating blight had dealt,
War, war ! its desperate terrors made
   Their din of death and anguish felt.

Ah, dear the victories that were won !
   For every hero who was lost,
A Rachel mourning for a son :
   A breaking heart to pay the cost.

Then, life and treasure lent their all,
   And half a people nobly braved
The martyr's destiny—to fall—
   That haply freedom might be saved.

Ah, martyrdom indeed was borne,
   Where homely men, undaunted, died,
Not knowing of the coming morn
   With all its fruits to them denied.

Their ardent souls could not recoil,
   And through the torturing struggle bore
Starvation and relentless toil,
   That earth might have one nation more.

A hundred years, and here we crown
   Their valor with our meaner praise.
Let, now, the reverence that we own
   Be written in our works and days !

A CHALLENGE TO WINTER.

Drift, drift, thou blustering sleet and snow,
And blow, thou trumpet-tempest, blow,
Shrill whistle through the caverned night,
To wake the hollow and the height :
   Blow, blow !

The winter's hoary crest is crowned ;
The fountain-heads and lakes are bound ;
The streamlets throb through fen and field,
Imprisoned in their icy shield :
   Ho, ho !

The grim north, through the star-lit sky,
Shoots its pale spire-lights far and high,
And thin and weird, the shadows trace
Ghost-lines across the glittering space :
   Cold, cold !

What care I for the crazy winds,
The storm-blast or the sleet that blinds ?
Away, ye wandering fiends of wrath !
Pile, pile the hickory on the hearth :
   Bold, bold !

Touch fire to its pent passion, cheer
And challenge the dead frozen year,
So heavenward shall the flaming dart
Pierce Winter to its icy heart :
   Ha ! ha !

Then stir the wassail, heap the fire,
Wake, drowsy pulse, and touch the lyre ;
Let the wild love-song throb and thrill,
To match the Arctic winds, and shrill :
   Hurrah !

REST.

O banish work ! Undo the prison door
 That holds the busy brain to drudging care !
 Has nature's largess no high gifts to share
With weary souls ? The waves that wash the shore,
The soft winds, soughing through the pines, the
  moor,
 The forest's stealthy trail, the rocky lair,
 The mountain peak, 'mid misty dreams of air,
The lonely haunts, where rippling streams restore
The echo of some matchless voice, and rhyme
 Perpetual music to the solitude,—
Or tune their lyrics to the lover-time—

Can these not win us from the mortal feud,
And turmoil of the burdened years, to leaven
The earthly thought with some fore-rest of heaven?

POET OF EARTH.

Oh, be not ether-borne, poet of earth;
Stretch not thy wings to such a cloudless height
As ne'er to know the darkness of the night,
As ne'er to feel the touch of grief or mirth
That lives in human sympathy, whose birth
Is longed for in this world of love and blight;
Thou, too, must drink of sorrow and delight,
Must taste the joy of hope, and feel its dearth;
God's service lies not out of reach, and heaven
Is found alone through lowly ministry;
Some souls there are whose dumb chords wait the breath
Of other souls, divinely gifted, given
To voice the deeper tones, and lead the way
To immortality, through life and death!

GRANT.

OBIIT, JULY 23, 1885.

I know not how to touch the chords
   For our great chieftain lying slain ;
   The sword that smote him bears no stain
Of earthly battle,—'twas the LORD'S.

What mighty conflicts he had manned !
   Not fitfully, in frenzied haste,
   As tempests sweep with sudden waste,
Then die along the desert strand ;

But calmly, through tumultuous ways,
   While brave men blanched, he led the van,
   With spirit of a stalwart man
Engraven on his Roman face.

The troublous days and years moved by ;
   The courage of the people waned ;
   The nation's noble faith was strained,
As victory seemed to droop and die ;

But he, the dauntless, centred there,
   Commanding the heroic host,
   Invincible where needed most,
At last moved forward, everywhere.

Then swiftly dawned the morn of Peace,
    Triumphantly, from walls of fire
    That stirred the nation's wild desire,
That shot their light across the seas.

And from his lips so prone to wait
    Till words were deeds, a message went
    In great laconic lines, that meant
A potence in the nation's fate.

And now, bereft, the legions stand :
    All mute, as one with bended head,
    A nation mourns beside the dead,
And silence fills the stricken land.

PROPHETIC.

The year, the year is passing—gone—
    Drearily cold the wind is moaning ;
The hoar-frost crowns the fields forlorn ;
    The trees, with icy fruit, are groaning ;
From ferny vale to mountain pine,
Death has written its countersign.

Time has touched with its fateful breath
    All the flowers that once were blooming ;
Alas, the issues of life are death ;
    Light is lost in the shadowy gloaming ;

Arch December, even so soon,
Follows the happy ides of June.

Lo, beyond the ominous sky,
  Hidden, the pulse of spring is beating ;
Upward the burnished sun mounts high,
  Painting the heavens with golden greeting,
Thrilling earth with its throbbing heart,
Piercing her with its fiery dart.

Out with thine idols turned to clay,
  Whate'er thou, Old Year, missed of bringing,
Waits in the weal of the coming day,
  Waits in the heart of the year beginning.
Ring, glad bells of the year to be !
Fulfil, O year, their prophecy !

SPIRITS ANEAR.

Not a word is said ; we sit by the hour ;
  And the twilight fades, and the shadows fall.
The perfume floats from the sleeping flower ;
  The birds have ceased to question and call.

Not a word is said ; our lips, they are dumb ;
  Her form is veiled, in the darkness, from sight ;
The pulses seem stilled, and the senses numb,
  Entranced by voices of nature and night.

None other is here ; we two are alone ;
    No outward token to give or to take ;
We gaze at the stars, and the fathomless zone,
    Till thoughts are deep with the fancies they wake.

We murmur a song, and our voices blend ;
    We dream the same dreams, though we know it not ;
Our spirits have learned the secret, to send
    Their messages each to the other's heart.

No protest, no vow can strengthen the bond ;
    O meaningless words, when silence is dear !
The converse of love is sweeter, beyond
    The shallow of speech, to spirits anear.

PAST THE PORTAL.

Falls the shadow on my sight :
Fade earth's glimmering spears of light ;
    Slowly, now, my vision, paling,
    Closes—all things outward failing—
        It is night !
It is night ! O night and sleep,
Fill my soul with silence deep,
        Night and sleep !

I have never felt it so,
In my slumbers here below ;
   Cold and still, heart-throbbing ceases :
   Strange ! my spirit life increases
      Its wild flow !
Is it night, and is it sleep
Sways my being's upward leap
      Through the deep?

Fly the shadows !   Lo, I feel
Rapture thrill ; and through me steal,
   All unfettered, dreams of longing—
   Swift emotions through me thronging—
      Lo I feel
Grief depart, and earth's dull sense
Take its flight ; O joy intense !
      Whither hence ?

Music ! aye, a thousand strains,—
Frees me from my drudging pains,
   Stirs me,—wreathes about my spirit ;
   Now I feel it, breathe it, hear it !
      Now it wanes—
Now it echoes near and far,
Floating on from star to star ;
      Near and far.

O what matchless radiance falls
On my soul, and inly thralls !

Bathes me in its passioned splendor,
Clothes me in its robes of grandeur,
    Inly thralls!
Light and music! Fly away
Death, with these thou canst not stay,
    Fly away!

How ineffable is this!
Full and free I drink its bliss—
  In the heavenly ether flying,
  Winged to feel the faint winds sighing—
    Feel their kiss—
Hear the eternal anthems sweep
To the rhythm of the deep—
    Mighty deep!

Take me, bear me in thy might!
Flee, thou dark, discordant night!
  Clouds, dissolve thy films of sorrow;
  Spirits need not of thee borrow,
    They are light!
Sink, thou dregs of eddying dross!
Perish wild despair and loss,
    Perish dross!

Infinite! I feel thy flow;—
Thy dim mystery I shall know,
  Thy unutterable spirit, dawning,
  Soon will crown the endless morning,

I shall know!
Cloud and shadow sink to night;
Angels flood Thy space with light;
All is light!

THE SOUL OF ART.

The sculptor, forward-gazing, deemed
    That, sometime in a golden year,
When art in him had touched the goal,
When life had ripened in his soul,
    His hand might celebrate the seer,
And carve the statue he had dreamed.

The statue, "Beauty." Lo, he saw
    It, fancy-drawn within his thought—
As he foretold, in curving line
Of Grecian grace, its fair design—
    And day by day, though still unwrought,
Beheld it fashioned without flaw,—

Love-fashioned; now it seemed complete,
    A child of passion, Venus-born;
The roseate hues of morning lent
Their flesh-tints to his rapt intent,
    And his dumb soul went out forsworn
To worship at his idol's feet.

Still, still his hands reluctant wait;
   The chisel by the untouched stone
His skilful fingers held, until
Some heaven-illumined sign should fill
   With deeper meaning than his own
The thought his art would consummate.

The years their circling courses traced:
   Mute as their rounds, his spirit changed;
More dimly shaped, within his mind,
The breathless form that love divined,
   Until his fancy seemed estranged,
His beauteous image half effaced.

And Time, at last, his glowing heart
   Through softening grades of feeling led;
It fused his passions till they blent
In sweet maturity, that lent
   A soul of harmony, and shed
A gentler fervor through his art.

Another beauty than of sense,
   Ideal—born of thought divine—
The soul's foreshadowing of Heaven—
Stole from his spirit, inward given,
   Like sainthood at the altar's shrine,
Reflecting its pure radiance.

And lo, a holier image rose
   From chastenings that his life had felt;

For sorrow, once—aye, thrice—had cast
Its darkness o'er him in the past—
   A darkness dense, wherein he knelt
To calm the storm of deepening woes.

And now the vision mastered him ;
   With patient chisel he expressed
The form, the master shape, that grew
Serene within his cloistered view—
   An image of his passion, blessed,
Pure as the templed seraphim.

To his grave face of marble came
   The voiceless song, the silent prayer,
The hallowed look, the crystal well
Of truth ineffable, to tell
   The character embodied there,
As moulded by a sacred flame.

Men paused and marvelled at the face ;
   Not fashioned from a fiery heart,
To thrill the veins and die anon,
But of celestial beauty drawn,
   Ennobling the noblest art,
Prophetic of immortal grace !

www.ingramcontent.com/pod-product-compliance
Lightning Source LLC
Chambersburg PA
CBHW030434190426
43202CB00036B/132